THE FREEDOM SHORTCUT

HOW ANYONE CAN GENERATE TRUE PASSIVE INCOME ONLINE, ESCAPE THE 9–5, AND LIVE ANYWHERE

MIKKELSEN TWINS

THE FREEDOM SHORTCUT

How Anyone Can Generate True Passive Income Online, Escape the 9–5, and Live Anywhere

Disclaimer:

Before we jump into showing you how to use the internet to create life-changing income streams that can pay you for the rest of your life, you need to understand one very important thing: There are no guarantees in life, so your results will be highly dependent on your efforts.

Although all the claims made in this book are truthful statements about results obtained by our customers, the results you're about to see are not average or typical. Why? Because most people don't do anything with what they learn. It's the same reason why people who buy a treadmill don't lose weight as a result of buying the treadmill. They lose weight as a result of using the treadmill and using it CONSISTENTLY over months and months.

Every successful person has put in the necessary time and energy into making this a life-changing endeavor. Every result here is real. There are no paid actors and no fake screenshots.

We strongly believe that any risk associated with following the steps outlined in this book is worth the reward.

For permissions requests, speaking inquiries, and bulk order purchase options, email: support@publishinglife.com.

ISBN: 978-1-7371424-5-4 | Paperback

Cover Design by Charlotte Mikkelsen
E-book Interior Design by Edward Fahy
Illustrations by Milena Ljubojevic
Editing by Lori Lynn Enterprises

Published in the United States of America

SOCIAL MEDIA PAGES

Mikkelsen Twins—PublishingLife

@mikkelsentwins

DEDICATION

I dedicate this book to my little growing family.

To my wife, Laura. I didn't know people as good as you existed before I met you. I will forever be in debt to you for all the sacrifices you've made to make my dreams come true. You treat me way too good. I love you.

To my sister-in-law, Charlotte. I often wonder what life would be like if we hadn't stumbled upon each other on a random hike in Maui. All I know is I'm very grateful that we did. Thank you for taking care of and making my brother very happy.

To my son, Finn. As soon as I started thinking about you and what to write here, my eyes filled up with tears. Words truly cannot explain how much I love you. Nothing comes close to how proud I feel when I get to say, "Yep, that's my son." All the sacrifices I make now are so that I can always be there for you and your future brothers and sisters.

To my twin brother, Christian. I was given an extremely unfair advantage over my competition when I was born with you as my twin. I want to write a lot more here because there's so much to say, but there's no need for that. I don't need to say anything for you to know exactly how I feel and neither do you. We just know.

—RASMUS MIKKELSEN

CONTENTS

MODULE 1: FOUNDATIONS

MODULE 2: CHOOSE

MODULE 3: OUTSOURCE

MODULE 4:
LAUNCH

MODULE 5:
MULTIPLY

MODULE 6:
DISCOVERIES

FOREWORD

Running an online business isn't always as glamorous and stress-free as it's made out to be.

I should know, because I tried almost every single one of them.

Selling physical products ... developing a mobile app ... running a local marketing agency ... freelancing.

Some made a little bit of money, but none were what was promised to me—the elusive "passive income."

Nearly all these businesses will have you working 10–12 hour days, cost seemingly endless amounts of money or time to get started with, and will provide you with unlimited frustrations.

I was about ready to give up.

That was until I found The Freedom Shortcut.

My name is Oliver El-Gorr, and I've been using the method taught in this book as my full-time income for four years now. On top of that, discovering this was the greatest thing to occur in my life.

It's given me more money than I could ever dream of. But more importantly, the freedom to travel and live all over the world and live life like the 1 percent.

Most importantly though, this was how I met the two gentlemen responsible for the book you have in your hands right now.

Let's rewind to what seems like a lifetime ago—2017. I was the fledgling newbie in yet another "How to Make Money Online" Facebook Group.

Everyone seemed to be crushing it, posting these huge numbers. But none of them were explaining *how* they were doing it.

None except a guy named Christian Mikkelsen, a 22-year-old kid from New Jersey.

Initially, I was jealous. After all, I was a wise 26-year-old who knew everything.

How dare someone a few years younger figure things out before me?!

But there was something different about this guy.

Not only was he posting huge numbers, but he was also willing to share the steps he was taking to get there.

Here was someone I could not only relate to but who was also pulling back the curtain on everything he knew.

That's how Christian (and his twin brother Rasmus) and I became acquaintances.

Since then, I've been fortunate enough to call them my friends, teachers, and mentors.

We've shared stages together. We've lived together on tropical islands. We've spent many hours debating who is the worst player in the entire NBA (I'm usually right, of course).

There are days when I feel like I have an unfair advantage over my competition just because of what I've learned from them. And I can safely say that I've never met two people more focused on changing people's lives.

They are stand-up guys. They wear their hearts on their sleeves. They don't hold anything back.

Frankly, there is no one better to learn this business from than Christian and Rasmus Mikkelsen.

Now, here is some advice I have for you when reading this book...

You're going to get excited. In the coming pages, The Twins are giving you the information and tools to change your life forever. This is no exaggeration or hyperbole. They are giving you the playbook to change the course of your financial future.

In fact, I'll go as far as to say that if you adhere to their teachings by the letter, it is impossible for you to fail. (Bold claim, I know.)

But I'm living proof of it, as are thousands of others who have been fortunate enough to learn from them.

Before you get there, though, there are probably a whole lot of "what ifs" going through your mind, certain preconceptions about the information contained in the coming pages, or maybe about the men delivering it.

I urge you to put those thoughts aside and approach this book with an open mind.

Because a long time ago, a mentor gave me a piece of advice that has stuck with me ever since. He called it:

"The Phenomenon."

It's the window of opportunity that you get once or twice in your entrepreneurial life ... where you have the ability to make more money in the next 12 months ... than you have in the previous 12 years.

And I want you to consider this book your personal "Phenomenon" moment.

So instead of filing this book away on the shelves with the rest of them, treat it like the key it is.

Whether you're a business veteran with 20+ years of experience under your belt ... or a bonafide beginner on Day 1 ... this powerful book shares the tactics and strategies to build a business that actually makes good on the promise of true passive income.

So grab yourself a cup of coffee, tea, or something stronger (I won't judge), strap yourself in, and discover what this world is all about.

—**OLIVER EL-GORR**
London, England

MODULE 1

FOUNDATIONS

FINANCIAL FREEDOM DOESN'T HAPPEN OVERNIGHT. BEHIND EVERY SUCCESS STORY IS A JOURNEY NO ONE SEES.

01

WHAT IS "THE FREEDOM SHORTCUT"?

Sweat is running down my forehead as I speed walk up the root-filled hiking trail, eager to finally lay my eyes on what we've been searching for all day. I wipe the sweat away before it reaches my eyes ... when I spot it in the distance.

I run up to the viewpoint and inch my way to the edge of the cliff to see it in all its glory.

There it is. Makahiku Falls. One of more than 100 breathtaking waterfalls in Hawaii. The flock of white birds circling the waterfall makes it feel like I'm standing right in the middle of a scene from a movie.

The others I'm hiking with catch up to me and stand right beside me staring at the waterfall, completely awestruck.

"I feel like I'm in *Jurassic Park* right now," says Christian, my twin brother.

"Well, the movies were filmed in Hawaii, so be on the lookout for dinosaur tracks," I said, checking to see if either of the girls were impressed by my witty joke.

No reaction.

Christian and I are standing there awkwardly, both trying to think of something cool to say to the two girls we had just met 20 minutes earlier on the hike.

"Sweet view, huh." I didn't know what else to say.

"Yeah, it is," says Charlotte. "Too bad my flight back to Canada is tomorrow. Then it's back to my job and reality I guess."

"What kind of job do you have?" I ask, doing my best to keep the conversation going.

She starts telling about her job as a graphic designer at a software start-up, but it quickly turns into an expletive-filled rant about her rude bosses and all the stress she's going through.

She says she used to enjoy design when she had the freedom to create things her way, but her bosses want everything done their way.

Now it's just turned into meaningless work that she doesn't enjoy anymore. Her bosses don't appreciate her, and she knows it's a dead-end job, but she says it would be hard to get the same salary working somewhere else.

"Cool, cool ... Well, that sounds like it sucks," I say. "Are you gonna do anything about it?"

"I mean, what am I supposed to do?" says Charlotte, "I don't get to decide. If I let them know how I really feel, then they'll probably just replace me, and I need to make money somehow. I should be happy that at least I can travel like this twice a year."

Every word she says resonates with me at my core because I remember feeling the same way.

It reminds me why I was so motivated to wake up early before school and stay up late after work to build my own online business.

I couldn't stand the idea of not being in control of my own life. I could never accept a life where I needed to ask another adult for permission to take a break from work or to go on a vacation with my family—a life where only two out of seven days were mine to enjoy, and the other five were spent working hard to satisfy someone else.

There are a few seconds of silence as Christian and I contemplate how to respond. Before we can, Charlotte breaks the silence. "Anyway, sorry for ranting about my problems at work. When is your flight back home?"

"We don't have a flight back," Christian says. "We live here."

"You live here?!" Charlotte asks, clearly surprised. "Sorry, you don't look like locals, so I just assumed you were from somewhere else."

"We're not locals. We're originally from New Jersey, but we moved here six months ago. We live in an apartment together in Honolulu right by Waikiki Beach, but in a few months, we'll be moving to Bali for the year," says Christian.

Charlotte has a puzzled look on her face as she's trying to wrap her head around what Christian just said.

"Are you serious?" she asks. "How is that possible?"

Christian explains how we've been making money online for almost two years, and as long as we have a laptop and a Wi-Fi connection, we can make money from anywhere in the world. No job, no boss, no office to show up at every Monday morning.

Whatever we want to do, we just do it, and we don't need to ask anyone for permission.

Charlotte's mind is blown.

"So you make money on the internet and you don't have a job. I don't understand. What exactly do you do?" she asks.

"Alright," I say, "so you know Amazon, right?"

"Of course."

"How about Audible?"

"Yeah," she says, "I use Audible all the time to listen to audiobooks. They're owned by Amazon, aren't they?"

"That's right. Let's just say that we found a way to set up many passive income streams on Amazon and Audible that pay us more than any job we've ever had before. That's how we're able to travel the world and work from anywhere."

"What do you mean by passive income streams?" she asks.

Christian butts in, "Passive income streams are things that make money, even when you're not actively working on them. To put it into perspective, I've made over $50,000 in the last six months doing this, and I haven't logged into my Amazon or Audible account once."

"You're telling me you make money even when you're not working?" She looks as if she's contemplating how that's even possible.

"Oh yeah. We've both been making money during this entire hike," I say.

Charlotte pauses, probably fantasizing about all the things she would do and all the places she would travel to if she could quit her job and work from anywhere in the world, too.

"I feel like you're wondering if you can do this too," I tell Charlotte.

She nods her head.

"One sec." I take the backpack off my shoulders, lay it on the ground, and unzip it. I reach my hand in and take out a mint condition copy of *The Freedom Shortcut* by the Mikkelsen Twins.

"Take this. It'll tell you everything."

Seven short months later, Charlotte is making full-time income doing the *exact* same thing as us. She quit her graphic design job, traveled to Bali to visit us, and ended up staying there for over six months living in our house. A little less than two years later, Christian and Charlotte got married in Hawaii on a Zoom call (thanks Covid) by a licensed marriage officiant.

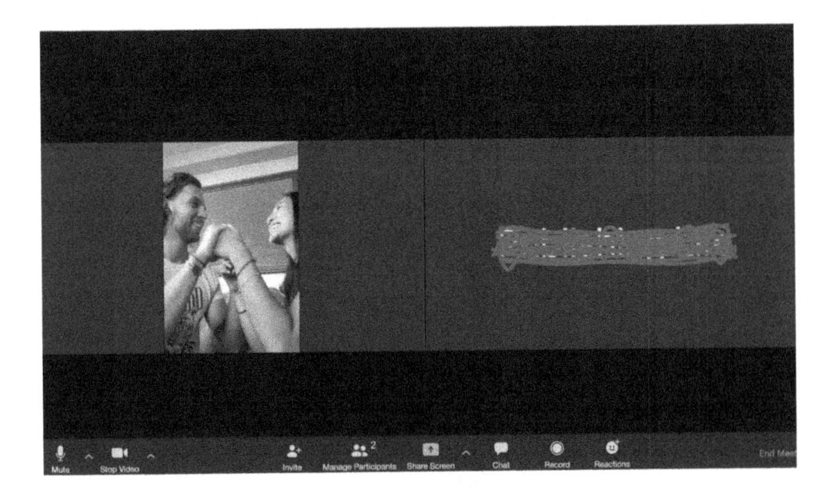

The ONLY part of that story that isn't true is when I pulled out a copy of this book and handed it to Charlotte. Although, if this book had existed at that time, that's definitely what would have happened.

Lucky for you, this book does exist now, and it leaks all the secrets that Charlotte used to replicate what we do, make passive income on Amazon and Audible, and quit her job in just seven months.

If you're at a similar place in your life where you're not satisfied with the lack of freedom you have at your job or the amount of money you make, then read this book to the end and apply the information because it can change your life faster than you ever thought possible.

The power this book holds is the equivalent to that of a college degree, except it'll take you months instead of years to start making money, you won't accumulate any debt, and the end result will be a life of freedom and autonomy rather than a life of being overworked and underpaid at a 9–5.

Financial freedom doesn't happen overnight. Behind every success story is a journey no one sees. Dive into the next chapter to find out how we started with nothing but an ambition to improve our lives and how we made our first dollar online.

02 HOW WE MADE OUR FIRST DOLLAR

The year was 2015 when I hit rock bottom.

Our parents always wanted us to live close to family, so we moved into a one-bedroom apartment in Aarhus, Denmark (Christian's bed was in the living room). We were born and raised in America, but only because our parents immigrated there two years before we were born. Our blood is 100 percent Danish, which probably isn't surprising because my name, Rasmus Mikkelsen, is as Danish as it gets.

All we had were high school diplomas, which doesn't get you more than a minimum wage job, but by some miracle, we both landed gigs as "manual labor specialists."

Our job was to unload shipping containers, and although it only paid minimum wage, at least the job title sounded impressive. We would show up at 6:30 a.m., put on our winter outfits and headlamps, and get assigned a container (either 20 or 40 ft). Then we would crack it open to reveal the mess of packages, sort them onto pallets, secure them with plastic wrap, drive it off with a forklift, and move on to the next container.

It was the most monotonous and unfulfilling work I had ever tried.

Here's a good test to see if you hate your job: If you're at work and you constantly check the clock hoping for the time to pass faster so the day can be over ... you hate your job.

Think about how sad that is.

I wished for time to speed up so the day could end. Every day, I wished for the day to be over. But every morning, it would just reset. The only thing that kept me going was knowing that a weekend would eventually come.

The thought that this could be my life for the next 30+ years, just like many of the other guys there, was frightening. Never mind that I'd be struggling financially my whole life with no ability to treat my future wife and kids with nice things. I just didn't want to hate five out of every seven days.

Anyway, we only lasted about four months there because we couldn't stand it. I find it funny how we didn't have the balls to quit or tell our parents, so we just stopped showing up one day. Good times ... Not.

We spent the next three months smoking pot every single day. My most significant responsibility had become choosing which show to binge-watch next on Netflix (I didn't want to let Christian down).

When our bank accounts eventually hit zero, we had to tell mom and dad. I was surprised by how little disappointment they showed. Looking back now, I think we set the bar so low that it was no surprise we couldn't hold down a minimum-wage job.

I spent months pushing away and suppressing all the negative thoughts I had about myself, but one night I couldn't keep it together anymore. I lay in bed and quietly cried myself to sleep.

I thought so little of myself. I had nothing to be proud of. We were just another expense for our parents (we needed them to cover rent for us) while providing nothing in return. I wondered what would happen if I died. Would people be sad? Probably not. I don't think anyone would even notice I was gone.

Since we had run out of money, our parents flew us home to live with them in New Jersey again. This was when I had to come clean to Christian about how I felt on the inside and that we couldn't continue being complete disappointments for the rest of our lives.

At the same time, our parents were putting pressure on us to enroll in community college. We both hated school our whole lives, but we agreed to it.

From the conversation with Christian and hitting rock bottom, we had both developed a fire inside. We were motivated to prove we weren't destined to be failures forever. College became that outlet for us. All the pent-up ambition we had, we directed it toward our college classes.

We both set a goal of achieving a 4.0 GPA in our first semester (4.0 is the highest grade possible for all the non-Americans reading this). We told our parents, and they thought it was a good joke. How could you blame them? We didn't know if we could do it, but we were ready to give it everything we had.

We got an email from the college six months later saying our first semester grades had been uploaded in the student portal.

ECO-211 60191 Economics I Macroeconomics	A	3.00			16SU5L
MKT-113 66205 Principles of Marketing I	A	3.00			16SU5L
BUS-112 46242 Intro to Business	A	3.00			16SU5E
HES-127 22806 Weight Training	A	1.00			16SP8L
BIO-101 23036 Anatomy and Physiology I	A	4.00			16SP16
CMP-110 20218 Intro to Data Processing	A	3.00			16SP16
ENG-112 20400 Composition II	A	3.00			16SP16
HED-286 20520 Personal Health & Wellness	A	3.00			16SP16
HES-125 21802 Stretching & Strengthening	A	1.00			16SP8E
ENG-111 80422 Composition I	A	3.00			15FA16
HED-115 83280 Personal & Family Nutrition	A	3.00			15FA16
HES-111 80552 Intro Exercise Science	A	3.00			15FA16
PSY-113 80975 General Psychology	A	3.00			15FA16
HON-PTK PTK HONOR SOCIETY	**	0.00			

Total Earned Credits	36.00
Total Grade Points	144.00
Cumulative GPA	4.000

I had earned 36 credits, 144 grade points, and had attained a 4.0 GPA.

That was one of the few proud moments I'd had up to that point in my life. And I promise you this was no feat of intelligence or natural talent. This was a matter of committing ourselves.

For the first time ever, we paid attention in class, we read all our notes from front to back twice a day, we went hard on every project and paper, and we completed every piece of extra credit. We stopped wasting our time with TV and video games and committed those hours to school work instead.

For once, we just tried really hard at something.

In the process, we both developed a feeling we had never felt before: belief.

Belief in ourselves and belief in our own abilities. We had just done something everyone said was impossible.

What other seemingly impossible goals could we also achieve?

We went into our second semester and did it again. Straight A's across the board for both of us. Going into our third semester, we were certain what was going to happen. And it did.

Suddenly, we went from people who failed at everything we tried to people that eventually succeeded at everything we tried. Notice how I said *eventually* succeeded at everything we tried. Because we still failed a lot—the difference was we would learn from that failure and try again, try again, try again until we eventually got it right. And this still rings true to this day.

We always manage to figure it out.

Five years ago, I could never have written this book. I'm the same person now, I've just developed a belief in myself that I *can* write this book. And so here I am writing it. But if I didn't believe I could do it, I'd never start.

Let me ask you this ... If you knew with 100 percent absolute certainty that you would make thousands of dollars every month on repeat if you just took action on what I'm about to show you in this book ... Would you do it?

Duh! Of course you would.

So why doesn't everyone do that?

Look at all the success stories from other ordinary people just like you and me (see Chapter 40). Whether the passive income model works is not the question for you. You know it works. The question is whether you believe YOU can do it.

As much as I hated community college and am still waiting to apply anything that I learned in the classroom to real life, it was worth it because it gave me belief in my own abilities. I didn't gain any skills, but because I genuinely believed in myself for the first time, I've been able to accomplish much more than I ever thought possible.

Let's say you told some Average Joe and me that we'd both be competing head-to-head in a Rubik's Cube competition in 30 days. The first time we both pick up that cube is going to look very similar. It's not going to make any sense, we're going to try different moves, and there will be no sign of progress for either of us.

As frustration rises, Average Joe believes it's only gifted or smart people who can figure it out. But I believe I can figure it out too. I just need some time to try things, make mistakes, learn from the mistakes, and try again.

It's not a matter of luck or skill. If someone else has done it, why can't I?

Although we had developed this incredible feeling of confidence, we were still broke and heading down a terrifying path, one that ends in us working 40 hours a week to make someone else's dreams come true.

You don't do that because you want to. You do that because they give you a paycheck, and you need that paycheck to get by.

I want to explore and experience life instead of asking for permission to take a vacation with my family. When I painted that picture in my head, I knew I could never go for that because I would never truly be happy. I'd be settling.

We learned the only path that would give us the freedom we needed to be happy was entrepreneurship. We can't have anyone else telling us what to do.

We figured being entrepreneurs wouldn't be easy, but it sure as hell would be easier than putting up with a corporate job for the next 40 years.

So while going to college full time and delivering Chinese food four days a week (Christian earned $10.25 an hour as a receptionist at a physical therapy office), we set off on our first entrepreneurial endeavor with 100 percent belief that we would succeed.

As twins, we had the genius idea that we would each try a different business model and whichever one found the most success, the other twin would jump over and join.

My first business: an online dropshipping store.

Christian's first business: self-publishing.

If you don't know what dropshipping is, it's where you sell physical products online by listing another company's products on your own website. Then when someone buys from your website, the company will ship the product to the customer and you get a cut of the profits.

After doing market research, the product I decided to sell was electric bikes. So I set up my website, contacted companies, set up payment processing, ran Google ads, did customer support, stayed up to date with inventory, created marketing videos, dealt with shipping issues, created social media pages, etc.

It was a lot. I was working my butt off just to keep this thing running.

I'll admit the first electric bike I sold was one of the coolest moments of my life. I had just taken an idea in my head, built it in reality, and made money with it, all by myself.

At the same time, Christian found this obscure business model called self-publishing. In a nutshell, the business model worked like this: You do market research to decide on a book topic, get a ghostwriter to write a book about that topic, get a book cover made for $5 to $10, then publish it directly to Amazon as an ebook and a print book with a few clicks.

We were very fascinated by the idea but still super skeptical. Afraid to risk any money, Christian decided to write his first book himself. He thought, *What the hell can I even write a book about?* After some pondering, he titled his book *How to Be a 4.0 Student in College, Like Me.*

Lame title, I know, but it was something. Two days and 5,154 words later, it was ready to publish.

Within 24 hours of it going live on Amazon, he made his first sale. Mind-blowing. It actually worked. He wasn't rich, but he was now equipped with everything he needed—six dollars and the confidence that he could repeat it over and over again.

Believe it or not, this short, unimpressive self-written book published in 2016 still sells a handful of copies every month and will continue to do so for many, many years. The two days Christian spent writing this short book has turned into multiple thousands of dollars in profit—and counting. Not bad.

After realizing the potential if he just repeated the process, he wanted to repeat it as many times as possible in the shortest period of time. The easiest way to do that would be to hire professional ghostwriters to write books for him.

Christian found some guy on Upwork (an online freelancing platform) claiming that he would research, write, and entirely create 10 books for him for the low price of $3,300. It was the deal of a lifetime!

In the one and a half years of living with our parents, Christian had saved up about $4,000 working as a receptionist and Chinese food delivery driver. Shortly after he sent over the $3,300, all communication was cut off, and he never saw that money again.

Devastating.

That was a powerful life lesson that I continue to be reminded of every time I try to take the easy way out: If it seems too good to be true, it probably is.

I think 99 percent of people would quit after being scammed online for the majority of their money. But he never considered quitting because we were both so frightened of what would happen if we didn't make this entrepreneur thing work.

The alternative was not a life worth living. We would make this work or die trying. Death is *literally* the only thing that could stop us.

So it took about three months to regroup and save up some money, but Christian was back in the game.

Over the following months, he slowly published more books, and his monthly income started to grow. Christian didn't write any of the books because he had ghostwriters do it for him. These were books about a wide range of topics. Some he knew very little about, but that didn't matter because the ghostwriter was very experienced within that topic.

While I was grinding away on my dropshipping store every morning before school and every night after work, I saw Christian do all the work at once to create and launch a book. He would never spend more time on that book, but it would keep selling month after month after month. I was working way harder, but Christian was making way more money.

So I had to publish a book too. I needed that first-hand proof that this would also work for ME.

Like Christian, the first book I ever published, I wrote myself. It was called *50 CrossFit Workouts to Get in the Best Shape of Your Life*.

I wrote it in two days, spent $10 on Fiverr for a book cover, then launched the book.

After 30 days, I had made $855 in royalties. No customer support, no fulfillment, no website, no social media pages. I just created the book, followed a simple launch strategy, and the book continued to sell over and over.

So I created three more books in the fitness niche (this time, I hired ghostwriters to write them for me) and turned my focus back to my dropshipping business.

Here is how my publishing and dropshipping businesses performed over the next six months:

	Time spent	Profit
Dropshipping business	30 hours/week (about 750 hours total)	$2,404.10
Publishing business	0	$9,337.01

While my dropshipping business was taking 30 or more hours per week (approximately 750 hours total), my publishing business took zero hours. After six months, the profit from my dropshipping business was $2,404.10, but my publishing business had brought in $9,337.01 in pure profit.

One business was taking all my time, while the other business that was just sitting there was making me more than three times as much money. It was obvious what I needed to do.

So I sold the dropshipping business in August 2017 for a nice $17,000.

Merchandise				
No.	Item Description	Quantity	Unit Price	Total Price
1	[illegible]	1	$17,000.00	$17,000.00
			Subtotal	$17,000.00
			Escrow Fee with concierge	($387.40)
			Total Transaction ID: [illegible] Escrow ID: [illegible]	$16,612.60
				All payments are in (USD)

Right after the sale of the business, we booked two one-way tickets to Thailand and never looked back. We removed all fall-back options and threw ourselves into the deep end with only two choices: sink or swim.

We had already grown our publishing income beyond what we needed to be financially independent, but we wanted more. We were hungry to grow our income past an average full-time salary. We wanted to be free and enjoy the nice things in life too.

We had our eyes set on $10,000 per month. That was the gold standard.

Since we already had a bunch of books out and selling, we looked for ways to make more money from the books we had. We knew audiobooks were a thing, but there were very few resources online showing you how to:

1) Get your books narrated and turned into audiobooks, and

2) get your audiobooks selling and making money.

Audible was the biggest seller of audiobooks at the time and they've done nothing but grow and grow and grow in popularity ever since. We were at the cusp of a life-changing opportunity and we didn't even know it.

Once we got into exploring the world of audiobooks, it was shockingly easy to do. It was as simple as listening to audio samples from different narrators, choosing the one we liked, and sending them the book manuscript. Then the narrator would speak the audiobook into existence.

One to two weeks later, they would deliver the audio files, we would pay them for their work, and that was it. Now we had 100 percent legal ownership of the audio files, and every penny made from selling these audiobooks would be ours to keep (besides the cut Audible takes).

When Christian's first audiobooks went up for sale on Audible, he didn't know what to do. He wanted them to sell more, but there was no one else teaching this stuff.

So, Christian did nothing. And his audiobooks started selling immediately. They didn't take off like wildfire, but they were making an extra few hundred dollars per month, and all he did was get it narrated and plop it up on Audible. It was too easy.

We knew audiobooks were on the brink of going mainstream. We could see there was no one else doing this stuff. This had the looks of a big opportunity, and we knew one of us had to double down on it.

So that's what Christian did.

You might be wondering why only Christian doubled down on audiobooks and not me too. Well, being the stupid twins we were, we still thought the best strategy was to test two different business models at the same time. To be fair, it did work out pretty well the first time we tried it.

So while Christian doubled down on audiobooks, I tried selling t-shirts online. Stupid, I know, but that's what happens when you don't know any better and you get distracted by every shiny, new opportunity you come across.

This book isn't about selling t-shirts, so you can infer how well that business worked out for me.

Anyway, Christian spent the next four months working on absolutely nothing but audiobooks. He locked himself in his room and didn't come out until the job was done.

He learned which topics sell really well as audiobooks, he learned how to optimize an audiobook listing, and he learned how to get his audiobooks in front of customers on Audible.

He cracked the code and his audiobook income skyrocketed.

Activity Summary Report acx

Christian Mikkelsen -

Report Type	Period	Beginning Balance	Current Period	Ending Balance	Amount Due
Digital Unit Sales Royalty	Feb-18		$2,207.13	$2,207.13	$2,207.13
Bounty	Feb-18		$575.00	$575.00	$575.00
Digital On-Demand Royalty	N/A*			$0.00	$0.00
			Withholding Tax	0%	
Grand Total		$0.00	$2,782.13	$2,782.13	$2,782.13

Activity Summary Report acx

Christian Mikkelsen -

Report Type	Period	Beginning Balance	Current Period	Ending Balance	Amount Due
Digital Unit Sales Royalty	Mar-18		$6,571.45	$6,571.45	$6,571.45
Bounty	Mar-18		$1,100.00	$1,100.00	$1,100.00
Digital On-Demand Royalty	N/A*			$0.00	$0.00
			Withholding Tax	0%	
Grand Total		$0.00	$7,671.45	$7,671.45	$7,671.45

He didn't publish another audiobook after March 2018 to focus his efforts on making videos for our new YouTube channel instead, but the money kept rolling in month after month after month.

Activity Summary Report acx

Christian Mikkelsen -

Report Type	Period	Beginning Balance	Current Period	Ending Balance	Amount Due
Digital Unit Sales Royalty	Apr-18		$8,436.96	$8,436.96	$8,436.96
Bounty	Apr-18		$1,850.00	$1,850.00	$1,850.00
Digital On-Demand Royalty	N/A*			$0.00	$0.00
			Withholding Tax	0%	
Grand Total		$0.00	$10,286.96	$10,286.96	$10,286.96

Activity Summary Report acx

Christian Mikkelsen -

Report Type	Period	Beginning Balance	Current Period	Ending Balance	Amount Due
Digital Unit Sales Royalty	May-18		$10,259.92	$10,259.92	$10,259.92
Bounty	May-18		$1,675.00	$1,675.00	$1,675.00
Digital On-Demand Royalty	N/A*			$0.00	$0.00
			Withholding Tax	0%	
Grand Total		$0.00	$11,934.92	$11,934.92	$11,934.92

Activity Summary Report acx

Christian Mikkelsen -

Report Type	Period	Beginning Balance	Current Period	Ending Balance	Amount Due
Digital Unit Sales Royalty	Jun-18		$6,833.40	$6,833.40	$6,833.40
Bounty	Jun-18		$1,100.00	$1,100.00	$1,100.00
Digital On-Demand Royalty	N/A*			$0.00	$0.00
			Withholding Tax	0%	
Grand Total		$0.00	$7,933.40	$7,933.40	$7,933.40

Activity Summary Report acx

Christian Mikkelsen -

Report Type	Period	Beginning Balance	Current Period	Ending Balance	Amount Due
Digital Unit Sales Royalty	Jul-18		$6,427.03	$6,427.03	$6,427.03
Bounty	Jul-18		$2,175.00	$2,175.00	$2,175.00
Digital On-Demand Royalty	N/A*			$0.00	$0.00
			Withholding Tax	0%	
Grand Total		$0.00	$8,602.03	$8,602.03	$8,602.03

Activity Summary Report acx

Christian Mikkelsen -

Report Type	Period	Beginning Balance	Current Period	Ending Balance	Amount Due
Digital Unit Sales Royalty	Aug-18		$5,743.85	$5,743.85	$5,743.85
Bounty	Aug-18		$2,500.00	$2,500.00	$2,500.00
Digital On-Demand Royalty	N/A*			$0.00	$0.00
			Withholding Tax	0%	
Grand Total		$0.00	$8,243.85	$8,243.85	$8,243.85

Activity Summary Report acx

Christian Mikkelsen -

Report Type	Period	Beginning Balance	Current Period	Ending Balance	Amount Due
Digital Unit Sales Royalty	Sep-18		$4,167.59	$4,167.59	$4,167.59
Bounty	Sep-18		$2,550.00	$2,550.00	$2,550.00
Digital On-Demand Royalty	N/A*			$0.00	$0.00
			Withholding Tax	0%	
Grand Total		$0.00	$6,717.59	$6,717.59	$6,717.59

Over the next six months, Christian made over $50,000 ($53,718.75, to be exact) and it didn't cost a second of his time or a penny out of his pocket. We had discovered how to make true passive income.

Since no one else on YouTube was talking about audiobooks, that became our thing. We became the go-to audiobook experts in the very small self-publishing community.

Publishing ghostwritten ebooks and print books on Amazon gave us the freedom to quit our soul-sucking jobs and travel the world. Then, audiobooks catapulted us to the next level and created our dream life.

For us, 2018 and 2019 were spent living in Hawaii and Bali. It was non-stop adventure, exploration, and unforgettable memories. For the first time in my life, I felt pure unconditional happiness.

Through this book, my goal is to pass that same experience on to you. Everything you need to achieve the same results as us has been distilled, refined, and packaged into this book.

Some may tell you that everyone in the world deserves to live a life of freedom and abundance.

Unfortunately, that's not true.

You aren't owed anything.

Lazy people don't deserve the same success as the go-getters.

I'm not saying it's going to be easy or it's going to happen overnight, but it's damn doable for anyone, even for two stupid potheads such as ourselves. You will need to work, but you already do that at your job for a paycheck. At least let your hard work go toward something that actually matters. Your f*cking freedom.

If you're serious about taking control of your life and your family's life, read this book to the end right now. It is a gift from heaven.

03

WHO THE F*CK ARE THE MIKKELSEN TWINS?

Our names are Rasmus and Christian Mikkelsen (or the Mikkelsen Twins for convenience). We are identical twins, best friends, and the founders of PublishingLife.com.

It's not so hard to tell us apart now, but we looked like exact replicas as kids!

When we spoke at the Self-Publisher's Cancun Mastermind in 2018, we were introduced as the "Pioneers of Audiobook Publishing" not because we were the first to do it, but because we were the first to popularize it and teach others how to do it too.

Back when we got started, there was no one else teaching this stuff. (If you see others teaching it now, they were most likely our students and learned from us.) Everything was learned through experience with no guidance, which isn't easy because it involved wasting a lot of time and money. But hey, we had no other choice.

Needless to say, it worked out, or else we wouldn't be writing this book!

Audiobooks gave us the freedom to fulfill our biggest dream—to see the world. We've swum with wild dolphins in Hawaii, strolled around the ancient pyramids of Egypt on camels, walked with Komodo dragons on the island of Komodo, visited the sacred temples of Japan, played with wild monkeys in Bali, skydived in Australia, cliff-jumped in Croatia, and seen Chichen Itza in Mexico (one of the seven wonders of the world).

I (Rasmus) have always said my goal is that when I die and we have the technology to analyze people's memories, I want the doctor to crack open my head and say, "Holy moly, this guy experienced everything great the world has to offer." Weird way of saying it, I know, but that's how I feel. I don't live for money or material things—I live for experiences.

Go to publishinglife.com/travel to see a photo album and video compilation of all our travels.

While publishing did a lot of amazing things for us, our life was far from perfect. We were still very shy and socially awkward. I had faced a lot of my fears, but one in particular scared the sh*t out of me. It haunted me every day because it was single-handedly holding me back from achieving the success I really wanted.

If you're familiar with our content on YouTube, then you've probably heard me talk about this before.

It was my fear of speaking on camera.

I was deathly afraid of it. I was worried about how stupid I would look, all the dumb things I would say, and what everyone else would think of me. *Why are Rasmus and Christian making YouTube videos? That's not the kind of people they are. They're so weird and awkward. How embarrassing.*

I couldn't handle the thought of others reacting that way, so for years, I curled up into my shell and kept pushing it away. Day after day, I continued to ignore this monster standing in front of me.

So I confronted it.

After the first filming session, which was so uncomfortable and full of tears of frustration, it felt like 10,000 pounds had been lifted off my shoulders.

When we posted our first incredibly cringe-worthy video on YouTube, I wish I could say all my worries were unfounded. But the truth is there was a lot of judgment from friends and family. It was very hard in the beginning, but eventually you realize that the opinions of others mean absolutely nothing.

We posted our first video about self-publishing on YouTube in April 2018 and had committed to doing a video every other day. No one watched in the beginning, but we kept putting out videos.

About 10 videos in, we started gaining about 1–2 subscribers per day.

As we continued to release more videos, it was always the videos about audiobooks that got the most interest from people. There was no one else on the internet talking about this at the time, so that's what we focused on. All our videos were just us showing how we were making money with books and audiobooks. The few people that watched our videos loved them.

When we first started our YouTube channel, we NEVER had intentions of selling an online course. We just didn't want to be those guys. But our subscribers started begging us for it. At that point, we felt it would be rude not to give the people what they want.

A few months and 90 YouTube videos later, we launched the first version of our online program, Audiobook Income Academy (AIA for short), to our small YouTube channel of 1,200 subscribers, and 96 people joined on the first day. That's where our journey as online educators/teachers started.

That transitioned into us creating PublishingLife.com, an education company founded to help people get out of the soul-sucking 9–5 life and into a life that freaking excites them—using the book and audiobook publishing business model.

Now our company is at the top of the education industry, we're a team of over twenty people, and we've been featured in business magazines like *Forbes* and *Entrepreneur*.

Google search "Mikkelsen Twins Forbes" or "Mikkelsen Twins Entrepreneur" if you're curious to read those articles.

What's in it for us?

Why are we leaking our secrets in a $20 book? Well, first of all, we're not selfish bastards.

Joking aside, my goal here is simple. I'd like to earn your trust. I know that if I can help you make money first, then you'll recommend this book to others, and hopefully, you'll come back to us for more in the future.

If not, I sleep incredibly well at night knowing I'm giving you much more than you paid for. It's a win-win.

Not to seem all selfless and noble, but it is incredibly gratifying when you can give the gift of freedom to others. When I found my freedom, you couldn't wipe the smile off my face for the first year (after that, it just became normal).

A student of ours, Christian D., made this post in our private Facebook group saying:

> *I have never been happier in my life. For years I hated every minute of every day. I had a job scraping rotten chicken grease and a dropshipping business on the side, totaling 70–80 hours a week. Publishing and AIA literally saved my soul. I feel a burning fire inside of me for life! When you truly love your work, you will stop counting the hours. I quit my horrible job and dropshipping, and I climbed to the top of a forestry ranger tower in a heavy storm on top of a mountain and felt the wind and rain and clouds hitting*

me in the face and felt tears of pure joy rolling down my face!!! I threw my arms up in the wind and felt free for the first time! Life is too short, chase your passion relentlessly as if your life depends on it because it does!

Through our premium program, we have helped thousands of people make their first dollar online, and hundreds of those people have turned that first dollar into full-time income (and much more as you'll soon see). In fact, many of our students have surpassed our own results with Amazon publishing. It just goes to show how incredible the business model is and how anyone can replicate it.

If you'd like to read more about these success stories, I've collected some screenshots and videos of these people sharing their stories and results. Go to publishinglife.com/success. In no way can I promise you results like these, but I want to show you what's possible when you take this and run with it.

Fast forward to today ...

We both live with our wives, splitting our time between Europe and America as we explore many travel destinations throughout the year.

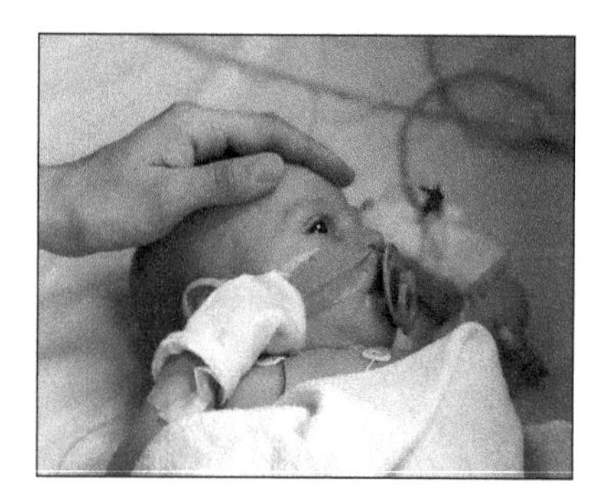

On June 30, 2020, my first son, Finn Raz Mikkelsen, was born. At two months of age, he was diagnosed with a rare and life-threatening liver condition called biliary atresia and was immediately sent into surgery.

This was, by far, the hardest experience of my life. We were told the surgery was not successful and that he would need a liver transplant to save his life. After many medical tests, I was deemed compatible to donate a part of my liver to him.

By some miracle, his condition slowly improved over the following months to the point where doctors have decided to postpone his transplant indefinitely. A transplant is still needed at some point in the future, but right now he is doing incredibly well.

This may be unnecessary to include in a book, but I want to share it because:

1) I'm proud of my son, and

2) our life isn't all sunshine and rainbows either.

Everyone faces hard times and adversity, and I'm no different.

It's also very important to me to remain the same person when I'm on camera, on stage, or writing a book as I am in real life. We get A LOT of flack for having a dirty mouth in our videos sometimes, and we've been asked hundreds of times to clean it up.

While I respect that our style of talk isn't for everyone, that's us being us. Some people love it, and some people hate it. We do our best to be considerate, but if we let other people dictate how we talk, then we just can't be our true selves, and we would only be acting like someone else every time we get on camera.

If we push some people away and make less money because of it, that's perfectly fine. It's much more important that we're comfortable being our true selves. When I'm speaking passionately about something, I can't help but let a bad word slip every once in a while!

THE ONLY WAY TO MAKE REAL PASSIVE INCOME IS BY BUILDING A MACHINE THAT MAKES MONEY FOR YOU.

04

WHO THIS BOOK IS FOR

Although anyone with a laptop and internet connection can build a profitable Amazon publishing business, the secrets shared inside this book are not for everyone. We've coached thousands of people in our online program, and there are certain types of people who consistently fail to create long-term income.

This book is not for people who:

- Want to get rich quick.
- Expect to make effortless earnings.
- Think making money online is a scam.

These are all behaviors that are conducive to failure.

If one of those categories above describes you, please take a moment to light this book on fire, throw it in the garbage, give it to your dog, put it in a paper shredder, or dispose of it in whichever way you would enjoy the most because it will be a complete waste of time for you to read it.

What we teach is not a get-rich-quick tactic you can exploit. It is predicated on using the power of Amazon and Audible to educate and provide solutions to people's problems at a profit through books and audiobooks.

Now, what is passive income?

Passive Income

[pa-siv in-kəm] noun

Income that requires no effort to earn and maintain.

Once we get into the step-by-step, I don't want any angry emails or YouTube comments saying, "Wait, I have to do work?! But you said this was passive income!"

It is passive income, but that doesn't mean you can sit on your ass all day doing nothing and expect your computer to magically start spewing money in your direction.

The only way to make real passive income is by building a machine that makes money for you. Then, no matter if you're sleeping or on vacation, this machine chugs away on its own, generating income for you 24/7/365.

Here's the catch: The machine has to be made *before* you can reap the rewards from it. But once it's made, you never have to build it again, yet it will continue to pay you for a lifetime.

This book is your step-by-step manual to building that passive income machine.

I know I just admitted that you need to do work to make this happen, but don't let that scare you. I have yet to find another model that requires less effort, money, time, and skill to be successful. And that's because I'm going to show you how to get professionals to do most of the hard work for you.

So who is this book for?

- Non-writers: We show you how to hire a professional writer for pennies on the dollar to write your book for you, so your writing ability plays absolutely no role here.

- People with no interest in books: THIS IS US! I occasionally listen to audiobooks now, but I could count on one hand how many books I had read from front to back when we first got started. You don't need to be passionate about books, you just need to be passionate about improving your life.

- People who have never started an online business before: Prior experience in business or books doesn't matter. A large portion of our most successful students had no prior business experience whatsoever.

- People who have tried to start an online business and failed: That was us too. Because this is all done with the help of Amazon and Audible, it's a very simple model with much less complexity than any other online business you may have tried.

- Business owners: If you own a business and you do not have a book to position you as an authority in your niche and generate leads, this book will help you do that.

- Authors: If you're an author who struggles to market and make full-time income from your books, this book will help you do that.
- Travelers: This business can be done from anywhere in the world with ease, all you need is a laptop and a Wi-Fi connection.

Ultimately, this book is for anyone who has a desire to make passive income and improve their life. If that's you, continue to the next chapter.

"IF YOU DON'T FIND A WAY TO MAKE MONEY WHILE YOU SLEEP, YOU WILL WORK UNTIL YOU DIE."

05

THE SECRET FORMULA

When we first got started online, we tried our fair share of different businesses. Some were complete busts, some we had moderate success with, but nothing even comes close to the consistent profits publishing brought in for us.

Many (if not most) of our students also had multiple failed online businesses, yet publishing was different for them. For Destiny, this was the sixth online business she tried, and it was finally the one that worked for her. She shared this in our private Facebook community:

When my first audiobook came out a year ago, I had no idea what this could/would turn into. I remember the feeling the day after my first audiobook went live and I kept obsessively and anxiously refreshing this page every hour until this number finally said "1" and I was so excited you'd think I'd won the Olympics. Then I refreshed it again and it said 2 ... and the number slowly crept up and went to double digits, then triple ... and I just got giddier and giddier.

Having unsuccessfully tried affiliate marketing, apps, blogs, ClickBank, niche sites, SEO, blah blah blah over a period of several years ... selling 14 units of anything online seemed like a pipe dream. So it's insane to me that over 14,000 random people I will never know or meet have purchased one of my products ... and this isn't even counting KDP! And I haven't published an audiobook in 7 months, but publishing royalties are the gift that keeps on giving.

I have lived in Thailand this year, lived like a queen in Bali, plus visited 6 other countries, went to 2 of my best friend's weddings, went to spend time with my cousin's newborn baby, went to a Tony Robbins event in Singapore ... all because I wanted to, all on publishing money.

When I hear people complain about their lives or their jobs, and I tell them about publishing, they just brush it off, and I'm like—YOU DON'T GET IT—you can have a NEW LIFE in 6 months. Stop complaining to me and just do publishing, lol.

Anyway, this post has gone on longer than I planned. I'm looking forward to refocusing on growing my business more for 2020 and multiplying these numbers tenfold, as I have barely scratched the surface and I'm just getting started.

So very grateful for this business and for two random kids on the internet (that's you Christian and Rasmus) for sharing it.

What's the secret formula? Why are people making consistent profits with publishing when they couldn't make other businesses work?

While I'd love to say that Christian and I do an immaculate job as teachers, that's not it.

The truth is the business model just works.
Here are 10 reasons why:

1) It's Amazon. Order fulfillment, shipping, customer support, returns, etc. You don't need to lift a finger because it's all done by Amazon. What an advantage it is to have all the intricacies of owning a business taken care of by someone else.

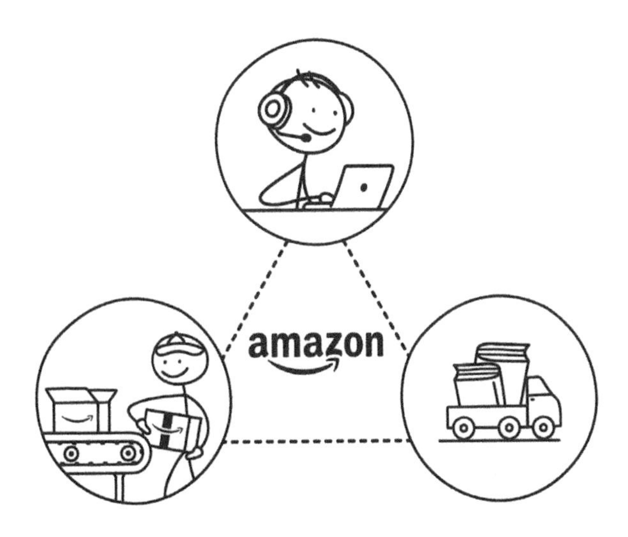

2) Audiobooks and ebooks are digital products, so it costs nothing to ship and you can never run out of inventory. It takes less than a second to zap an ebook or audiobook to a customer's phone or Kindle device, so whether you sell one book a day or 1,000 books a day, it's the same amount of work for you.

While print books aren't a digital product, Amazon uses a fully automated Print on Demand (POD) system where a book is only printed and shipped after someone purchases it. That way, there are no upfront costs and you never have to buy and store your physical books in a warehouse. So even with print books, it's completely passive and you can never run out of inventory.

3) A book only needs to be created once. After it's been written, narrated, and the cover is designed, then you can sell it and get paid until the end of time with little added effort. The first books we published in 2016 still make us money to this day, and I haven't even given them another thought.

Here's a fun fact: In the year 2020, thirty-three years after his death, Dr. Seuss sold over 6 million book copies.[1] He

---

1 Madeline Berg, "The Highest-Paid Dead Celebrities Of 2020," Forbes (Forbes Magazine, May 1, 2021), https://www.forbes.com/sites/maddieberg/2020/11/13/the-highest-paid-dead-celebrities-of-2020/.

wrote his books once, and now they will never, ever stop selling. That's real passive income.

If you have a service-based business or you sell a physical product, you have to continuously put in resources to deliver that product or service to your customers again and again.

4) So many different income streams can be created from just one book. You can sell the book in different formats (ebook, print book, and audiobook) on Amazon *and* on Audible *and* on many more book platforms outside of Amazon. There's yet another passive income stream you can create from your books with little effort that I have yet to mention, but I'll talk all about that in a later chapter.

5) A good book is the ultimate form of education and can make a significant impact on other people's lives. We're not just selling phone cases for a profit—real people are reading these books and positively benefitting from them. Good books have the potential to change lives; just look at Bill Gates and Elon Musk, who credit a big part of their success to reading books.

Publishing your own book is something that's on almost everyone's bucket list, but most never see it through because, truth be told, writing isn't easy. What most don't know is that you don't need to write the book yourself! You can be the brains behind the book, but you don't need to do the hard work. Leave that to the professionals who love writing and can do a way better job than you (no offense). Once you get to hold your own book in your hands, it's one of the most rewarding experiences in the world.

6) Publishing is fun. Why? Because you can create books about topics that you love. Even for the most niche topics, there are hundreds of thousands of buyers worldwide. A student of ours pays his rent from one book he published about Rubik's Cube. You'll see a ton more examples of super small niches that can make really good money in later chapters.

There's little competition compared to most other business models. Most people think selling physical products is the only way to make money on Amazon, and that's why there are so many people doing it. In fact, there are 300 million different products for sale on Amazon. Do you know how many audiobooks are for sale on Audible? Only 245,000. That means there are 1,200 products for sale on Amazon for every one audiobook that's for sale on Audible. (NOTE: These figures are taken at the time of writing and will change over time.)

7) Audiobook sales are booming and taking over the publishing industry. According to the Audio Publishers Association, "U.S. audiobook sales in 2019 totaled 1.2 billion dollars, up 16% from the previous year, with a corresponding increase in units. This continues the EIGHT-year trend of double-digit revenue growth."[2]

That means audiobook sales have grown by at least 10% every year for the last eight years. Sales numbers for 2020

---

2 "Americans Are Listening to More Audiobooks Than Ever." Audiobooks Continue Their Market Rise with 16% Growth in Sales, Audio Publishers Association, June 8, 2020, www.audiopub.org/uploads/pdf/2020-Consumer-Survey-and-2019-Sales-Survey-Press-Release-FINAL.pdf.

are yet to be released, but all indications point to another year of double-digit revenue growth with no signs of slowing down.

There were also 750 million print books sold in 2020, an 8.2% increase from the year before and "the highest year-on-year increase since 2010."[3] No matter how technology evolves, it seems there will never be a replacement for that new book smell and feeling the smooth paper and weight of a book in your hands.

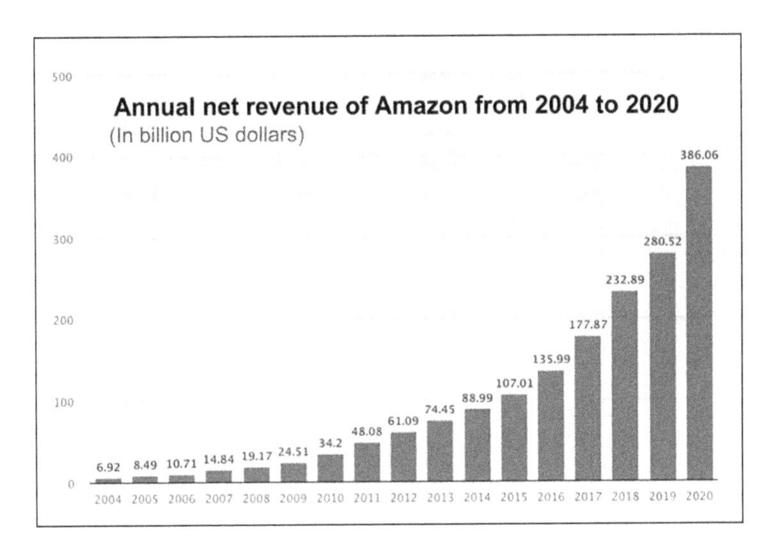

Online shopping is exploding as well. Due to the worldwide pandemic, people have practically been forced to shop online, and everyone selling on Amazon is winning because of it. If you're not at least selling something on Amazon, you are losing out.

---

3 Amy Watson, "U.S. Print Book Sales 2020," Statista, January 22, 2021, https://www.statista.com/statistics/422595/print-book-sales-usa/.

8) Lastly, this business model just works because it may be the only one you can find that is *truly* passive. If you feel like you deserve a break from work, you can take time off and feel comfortable knowing your books will continue to sell without you. If you want to go to sleep for six months, you can do that and feel great knowing that your books will be selling on autopilot while Amazon basically runs the business for you.

To quote one of the richest men in history, Warren Buffet:

> "If you don't find a way to make money while you sleep, you will work until you die."

Amazon book publishing is the simplest way for anyone to get started making money in their sleep, literally.

"DO WHAT YOU DO BEST AND OUTSOURCE THE REST."

06

THE FREEDOM SHORTCUT EXPLAINED

Another day, another mind-blowingly beautiful sunset in Bali, Indonesia. It's about 80°F, and we're waiting outside for our Go-Jek (Indonesian Uber) to take us to dinner.

The driver arrives, and we hop in the car. He's very good at speaking English, as many Balinese locals are, and is the type of driver who loves to talk.

"Hey, nice to meet you guys! How long are you in Bali for?" the driver asks.

"We actually live here. We've been here for six months now," I say.

"Wow, that's great! So what do you do for work?"

"We sell books and audiobooks online."

"Oh, you're writers! That's very cool."

We both laugh to ourselves, flattered that he had mistaken us for professional writers.

"Definitely not. Far from it," Christian says. "We don't write our books ourselves. We hire professionals to do that for us. We just publish the books and audiobooks and get sent the earnings at the end of every month."

"You can do that?! But you have to split profits with them, right?" he asks.

"No, they work for a one-time fee," says Christian, "so I own the book 100% and only split profits with Amazon."

"So you're telling me you literally have no writing skills, yet it's what you do for a living and how you're able to live in Bali?"

"Exactly!"

He didn't say that last part, but that's precisely what it is. Writing skills are not a part of the equation, only a willingness to do the steps.

You may be thinking, "If I'm not doing any of the heavy lifting, what's my role in the business?"

Technically, you're the owner, but I like to compare you to a chef. It's your job to find all the best ingredients and put them together. They are all right there at your disposal on the internet.

Here are the three main ingredients that go into a profit-churning book and audiobook publishing business:

1) Written Manuscript

2) Book Cover

3) Audio Narration

That's all it takes to publish books and audiobooks that generate sales and income every month.

> "Do what you do best and outsource the rest."
>
> —Peter Drucker

That is our philosophy. Hire professional writers, cover designers, and narrators to create an excellent book for you that can rightfully stand alongside other best-selling books on Amazon.

Typically, hiring professionals isn't cheap, but when you've been in the game as long as we have, you know exactly where to find all the most affordable talent. I'm talking so cheap that anyone could afford it just by cutting back on beers and date nights for a short period of time.

Now with these three ingredients, you can publish your book in three different formats:

1) Ebook

2) Print Book

3) Audiobook

From now on, when I say "book publishing," I'm referring to all three formats.

Each format is an income stream of its own as they sell mostly independently of each other. The ebook and print versions of your books will be sold on Amazon.com, and the audiobook will be sold on Audible.com.

The amount you make per sale varies on how you price your books, but it's about $2 to $3 for an ebook sale, $7 to $10 for a print book sale, and about $5 for an audiobook sale.

Please promise me, no matter what, that you will never publish a book in just one or two formats. That would be the equivalent of saying "No thank you, I don't want it," to free money.

When your book is published, it will be listed for sale on Amazon and Audible to the millions of people searching for books and audiobooks every day. But for someone to buy your book, they need to be able to find it first.

Let's say someone is expecting a new puppy and they want a comprehensive guide about how to raise a puppy. They would go on Amazon or Audible, type in "how to raise a puppy," and a selection of books would appear. The closer your book ranks to the top, the more your book will be seen, the more your book will sell, and the more money you will make.

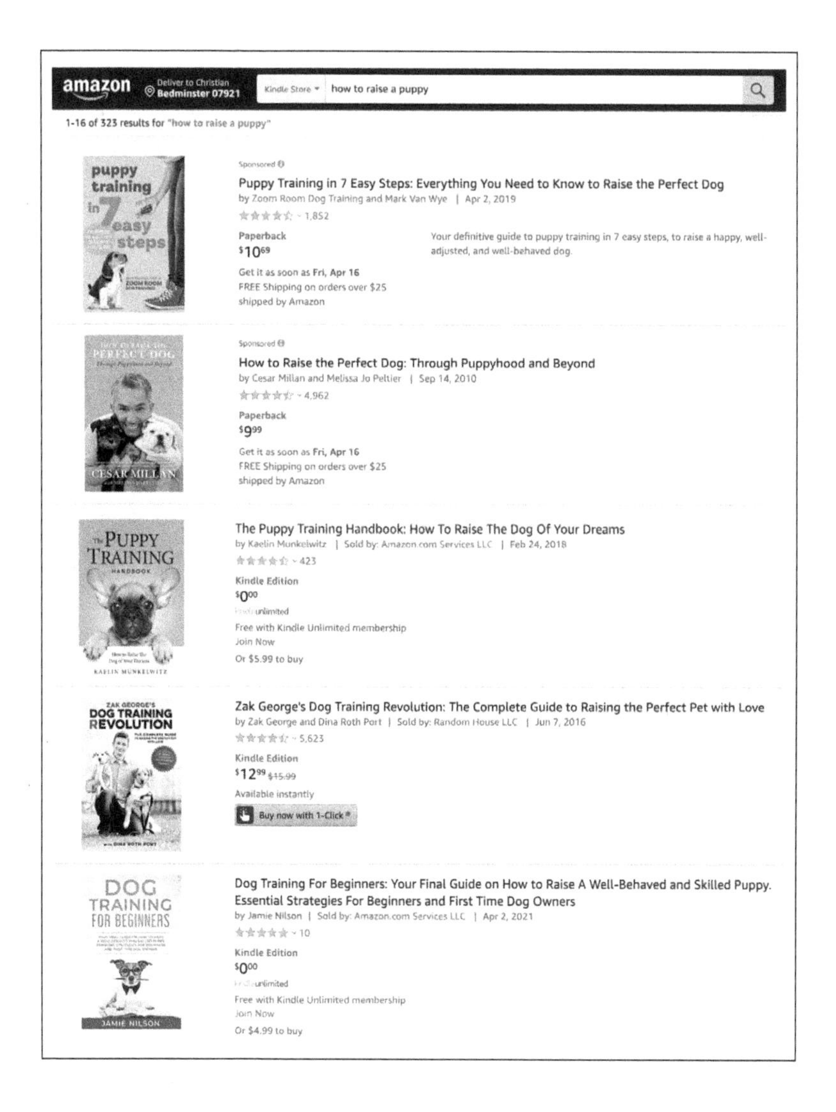

Where your book ranks has nothing to do with fame or some other element that's out of your control. It comes down to two factors: keywords and reviews, both of which you have complete control over. These are very important when launching your book, which we'll cover later in Module 4.

Once your book is published and ranking, well, there's not much else to do. The next step is to move on to the next book adding income stream after income stream until satisfied. Seriously, Amazon handles all the rest. This is how Christian made over $50,000 in six months without logging in to his Amazon account once. He built a portfolio of income-generating books and just waited for time to pass.

That's *The Freedom Shortcut* in a nutshell. It's using what you have in your hands right now! Oh, the irony.

We hire professionals to create our written manuscript, book cover, and audio narration for us. Then we package it together into an ebook, print book, and audiobook that we list for sale on Amazon and Audible and keep all the profit for ourselves.

It's a very simple business model. In later chapters, I will be diving deep into all the step-by-step how-to. This was just an overview.

BECAUSE WE'RE THE FIRST ADOPTERS AT THE START OF A GLOBAL TREND, THERE IS VERY LITTLE COMPETITION SELLING AUDIOBOOKS.

07

A NEW AMAZON PLATFORM

Audiobooks have disrupted the book industry. Every year, more and more readers are making the switch to audio, which has opened up a blue ocean of opportunity for anyone who wants to take it.

Someone who has taken this opportunity and run with it harder than anyone else is fellow publisher and AIA student, Patrick Jackson.

Instead of retelling Patrick's story, I want you to hear the words straight from his mouth. He wrote and shared the following in our Facebook community:

I want to say thanks to the twins for changing my life (and my lifestyle). I hope my story will inspire someone to have the same or even greater success than I've had. My story began in 2004 when I started

my first online business. I turned my hobby, which was learning foreign languages, into an online business. With the help of native-speaking foreign-language instructors who I hired from Craigslist.org, I created downloadable MP3 courses and CDs teaching people Spanish, Italian, and Portuguese. I sold the products from my website. It was much easier in 2004 because there was very little competition online. In my first year, I made just under $250,000. In 2008, I pursued my dream of living the life of an ex-pat and moved from my home in New York City to Medellin, Colombia.

But each year, as more and more people started online businesses, it became harder and harder to make money selling from my website. When I first moved to Medellin Colombia in 2008, I rented a fully furnished duplex in one of the best neighborhoods of Medellin. But by 2016, things had gotten so tough for my business that I found myself living in the hood in Medellin. I was the only American living in my entire neighborhood. By then, I couldn't afford to live anywhere else but the hood. The only thing I could afford to eat was rice, beans, eggs, and avocados. I went from making $250,000 in 2004 to making about $500 a month in 2016. Things were so bad for me that from 2016 to 2018, I could not even afford to purchase a plane ticket to fly to the USA to see my family and friends.

I had known about Audible for many years, and in 2016, I decided that I had nothing to lose and took the MP3 courses I was selling on my website and started selling them on Audible. But nothing changed! Instead of making $500 a month from my website, I was now making $500 from Audible. And then in the spring of 2018, I discovered the twins on YouTube. And within a year I went from earning $500 a month to my best month ever on Audible: $91,731.22.

> *Not only did I make enough money to finally buy a first class plane ticket to visit family and friends in the States in 2019, but I also took my dream vacation to Asia and visited four different countries: Thailand, Vietnam, Cambodia, and Indonesia. And I no longer live in the hood in Medellin. Once again, I am living in a penthouse in one of the best neighborhoods of Medellin. I have now sold close to 130,000 audiobooks on Audible—all thanks to the twins.*

If you want to watch a video of Patrick telling his story or listen to an interview with him, then go to publishinglife.com/patrick.

So how did Patrick go from making $500 a month on his own site to over $91,000 in one month selling on Amazon/Audible in such a short period of time?

Since he was already selling language learning MP3 courses and CDs on his website, he was very quickly able to take the audio files, turn them into over a dozen audiobooks, and put them for sale on Audible.

While he did have initial success selling on his own website, it fizzled out quickly because of one big problem: No one could find his site to buy his products. Millions of people are searching every day for products to help them learn Spanish, Italian, and Portuguese, but he couldn't get in front of those people.

Creating a good product to sell is the easy part. The hard part is getting customers for that product.

How many times have you seen someone create a website selling t-shirts, jewelry, watches, soap, etc.? They finally launch the store and ... *crickets*. Two weeks pass and not even a single sale.

Maybe you've done this yourself. You check your analytics and get excited to see that you had three people visit your site to-day. Sweet! And then you realize those three people were your mom, your dad, and you.

Patrick was going through the same trouble until he turned his MP3 courses and CDs into audiobooks and moved them all over to Amazon and Audible. Then, getting his books in front of customers became the easy part. Before searching for "how to learn Spanish" on Audible and then finding his audiobooks, 95 percent of Patrick's customers had never heard of him.

Although Patrick sells his audiobooks as ebooks and print books too, the vast majority of his earnings have come from his audiobooks. Why is that?

Well, his particular niche is tailored for audio because language learning is most effective when you can hear how the words are spoken and how they are pronounced.

But there's a bigger factor at play. There is a worldwide be-havioral shift happening where people are making the switch to listening to books instead of reading books. It's even re-flected in Amazon's slogan for Audible: ***"Listening Is the New Reading."***

The soaring popularity of audio can be attributed to people's desire to be more efficient with their time. You can listen to an audiobook while you're driving, cleaning, working out, or doing the laundry. What we're seeing is a universal trend that has just begun.

It's no surprise why Audible has been growing explosively since 2015. Audiobooks are the online gold rush of this decade.

On the flip side, it's trends like this that explain how Patrick and many other audiobook publishers are profiting massively. And because we're the first adopters at the start of a global trend, there is very little competition selling audiobooks on Audible. It truly is minuscule when you compare it to selling physical products on Amazon. Let me put it into perspective.

Products for sale on Amazon:

300,000,000

Books on Amazon:

48,000,000

Audiobooks on Audible:

245,000

For every one audiobook for sale on Audible, there are 196 books for sale on the Amazon book store and 1,224 products on Amazon.

So how is Patrick really making so much money?

By moving his audio content over to Amazon and Audible, he is harnessing the enormous amount of free traffic on Amazon and exploiting the minimal levels of competition selling audiobooks on Audible.

Imagine what Patrick's life would look like today if he had put his audio content on Audible at the same time he put it on his website back in 2004. Imagine how things would have been different for him if he knew how to get the kind of traffic that he's getting now.

In business, there's something called "Opportunity Cost," and it's essentially what it costs to miss an opportunity. For two years of his life, Patrick missed opportunities to visit his family. He missed opportunities to travel. And it cost him hundreds of thousands of dollars in missed income. If he hadn't taken what he learned from us three years ago and implemented it, he would likely still be living in a dangerous neighborhood that he could barely afford with no ticket out.

Audiobook publishing + this book to guide you = your ticket out.

THE PITFALLS

I'm not going to sit here and preach Amazon and Audible publishing to be absolutely perfect in every way with no drawbacks whatsoever—the perfect business model where you have to do no work, you don't need to invest any money, and your laptop is just going to print money forever.

That's obviously not the case.

There are drawbacks to this business model that you should be aware of. These are not to discourage you, I simply want to be transparent and for you to be fully informed before going all in. Keep in mind, I still believe Amazon publishing to be the easiest beginner-friendly business you can start with no skills and little start-up capital.

The four main drawbacks of Amazon publishing:

01 **You will not get rich quick.**
The reason for this is obvious. It takes time for a writer to write your book for you! That can't happen in a weekend, and if it does, I'd be highly suspicious of your

writer. Expect it to take about four to six weeks for a good, full-length book to be written.

A study from Stanford in the 1960s called "The Marshmallow Experiment" proved that seeking instant gratification (in this case, quick results) is detrimental to success in almost every area of life.[4]

How the study worked is they took 32 kids (16 boys and 16 girls) between the ages of three and five. They sat them down in an empty room, put a marshmallow on their plate, and said, "You can eat this marshmallow now, or if you wait 15 minutes, I'll give you another one." Kids being kids, most of them decided to eat the one marshmallow right away. But a handful of kids decided to wait the 15 minutes and get the second marshmallow.

They conducted follow-up studies with these 32 kids every few years to track how they were doing. The handful of kids who showed the patience to wait had higher self-esteem, they scored higher on the SATs, and they were less likely to be overweight. Generally speaking, they were more successful in every area of life.

This experiment proved that delaying gratification, being patient, and having a long-term mindset is a powerful predictor of future success. Everyone seems so eager to make money next week, and if it can't happen that quick, well, then it's not worth pursuing.

You must remember that in publishing, time is an asset, not a liability. Books continue to sell long after you put any work in,

---

4 A. E. Navidad, *"Marshmallow Test Experiment and Delayed Gratification,"* Simply Psychology, Nov. 27, 2020, https://www.simplypsychology.org/marshmallow-test.html.

so it is over time where the earnings really start to stack up. Be patient and reap the rewards.

I will say there is actually a way you can profit from publishing in the next 24 hours, but it's a bit unorthodox, and you're not ready for it yet.

And remember, time is relative. Compared to the usual "college–get a job–retire at 65" life path, making money with publishing goes VERY quick.

02 **You will need to invest money.**

In this business, you always have two options. You can either do it yourself (it's "free" but will cost you time and energy), or you can pay someone else to do it for you who will do it way better than you could have done it yourself (not free, but will cost you much less time and energy). Unfortunately, there is no magical third option where you pay nothing and do nothing.

I value my time more than anything else and will choose to hire someone to do the hard work for me every time. I suggest you do the same unless you enjoy being inefficient. In that case, go crazy working your butt off to save a few dollars.

So, while getting a profit-producing book made costs money, would you invest $600 in getting a good book written if you knew it could make you $600 every month for years? That's the easiest decision in the world.

Don't be one of those freebie seekers afraid to put money into anything because you're scared you'll never get it back. They're the friends you catch up with every year that are always stuck in the exact same position they were in last year.

And yes, there is still a way you can publish books without spending a penny. Does it require more work on your part? Yes, of course, but it's a lot less than you think and doable by anyone with a little bit of fortitude. Whichever way you choose, there are no excuses.

03 Publishing probably won't make you a millionaire, but it'll make you FREE.

Think about it though. Is making millions really the key to happiness? I can tell you from personal experience that it's not. The most joy I ever felt was during the years I spent traveling around the world and really experiencing life at its pinnacle.

You likely want to be a millionaire because of the lifestyle you think it gets you. What you're forgetting is that freedom is the sacrifice for making millions.

Sign me up for $5,000–$10,000 per month in truly passive income and all the free time I could ever want. With my books and audiobooks, no matter what happens, I know there will *always* be a direct deposit into my bank account at the end of every month (not even a pandemic can stop that from happening).

So how much can you realistically make? We have a big handful of students who we've helped make over $20,000 per month, so let's say that. Nonetheless, don't expect millions, but that's the trade-off for something being incredibly low risk.

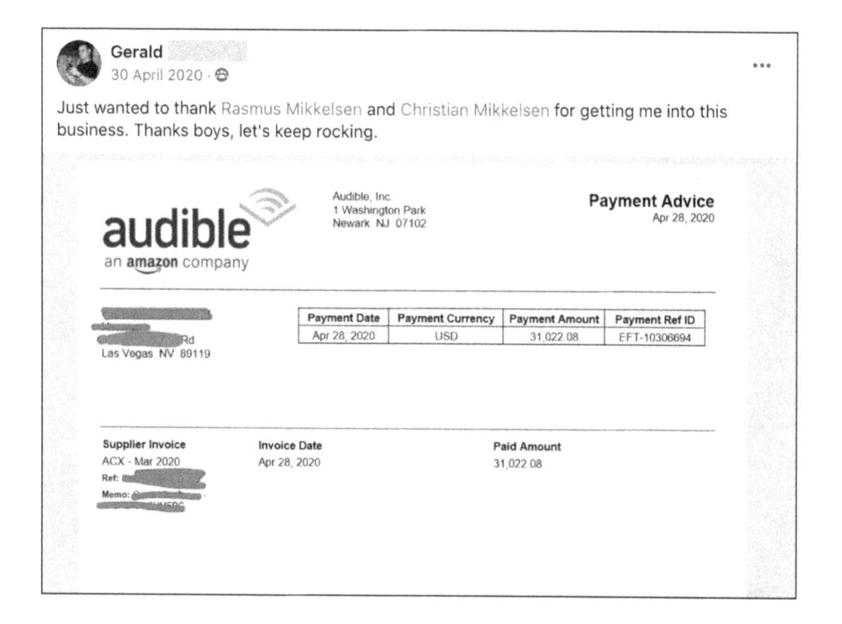

Gerald
30 April 2020 ·

Just wanted to thank Rasmus Mikkelsen and Christian Mikkelsen for getting me into this business. Thanks boys, let's keep rocking.

audible
an amazon company

Audible, Inc.
1 Washington Park
Newark NJ 07102

Payment Advice
Apr 28, 2020

Rd
Las Vegas NV 89119

Payment Date	Payment Currency	Payment Amount	Payment Ref ID
Apr 28, 2020	USD	31,022.08	EFT-10306694

Supplier Invoice	Invoice Date	Paid Amount
ACX - Mar 2020	Apr 28, 2020	31,022.08

Ref:
Memo:

04 Publishing on Audible is only available to people in the US, UK, Canada, or Ireland.

If you want to publish ebooks and print books on Amazon, you can do so from anywhere in the world with no exceptions, and that in itself is a worthy pursuit. But as you know, there's a lot of money to be made by getting your books narrated and turned into audiobooks and putting them on Audible.

Because of tax regulations, the publishing platform for Audible called ACX (short for Audiobook Creation Exchange) only allows people who are from or live in the US, UK, Canada, or Ireland to use their platform. So, if you're from one of those four countries, then you have nothing to worry about.

This is actually a good thing because it means fewer people are able to publish on these platforms. And fewer books means less competition!

THE BIGGEST MISTAKE YOU CAN MAKE IS NOT HAVING SOMETHING OUT AND SELLING, MAKING YOU MONEY PASSIVELY EVERY MONTH.

HOW TO NOT FAIL

Christian and I were doing one of our group coaching calls that we do with our AIA students every Monday. On those calls, people can ask questions, share their progress, suggest topics for us to discuss, ask for help ... anything.

Alex, one of our students, said he had created his first book and wanted to launch it this week. He wanted assurance that he didn't do anything wrong, so he asked if we could review his book and tell him what he's doing right, what he's doing wrong, and what he should change before publishing it.

We said, "of course," and I asked him to send his book cover to me. I threw it up live on the call for everyone to see:

I read his book title out loud: *Master of Pi: Memorize the First 10,000 Digits in Record Time. Unlock Your Brain, Learn the Power of Pi, and Discover Your True Potential.*

We sat and stared at the cover for a while as we formulated our thoughts on the book.

"Can you explain what this book is?" I asked.

"It's to help people memorize the first 10,000 digits of pi. It's a short introduction chapter in the beginning along with some memorization techniques, and then I just listed the first 10,000 digits of pi," said Alex.

"That's interesting ... I'll be honest, this is the first time I've ever seen someone publish a book about pi. When doing your niche research, how did the demand and competition numbers look?" I asked.

"Umm ... uhh, I don't know. I saw there weren't any other books about this, so I figured it was a good idea," said Alex.

"Ok." I didn't really know how to explain it to him. "I can see there's no one searching on Amazon or Audible for books about pi. To be honest, I don't even know who would want to buy this book or how they would even find it."

Alex didn't say anything.

"So did you quickly write this yourself, or did you pay a writer to write this for you?" I asked.

"I paid someone $250 to write it for me."

"Ok, look, I'm only telling you this to help." Then came the hard truth. "First of all, you chose a book topic with literally zero demand. Second of all, your book cover is underwhelming, the title could be much better, and it's something you could have easily written yourself in a couple of hours. You didn't have to pay someone $250 to write this."

Alex paused, not knowing what to say. "So should I still publish the book?"

"I mean, yeah, it's already done so definitely still publish the book. Just put it up, get some reviews, and move on to the next one. See it as a learning experience and move on."

Since he was so excited to publish his first book, that was a tough pill for Alex to swallow. Now it felt like he had been punched straight in the gut. He was extremely disappointed and discouraged by the feedback we gave for his book, but he trusted what we said. He launched the book later that week and moved on to the next one.

Ten months later, I randomly thought of that pi book again and, just out of curiosity, sent a message to Alex asking how sales for that book have been.

"It flopped just like you said it would lol," he wrote back. "It sells maybe a few copies every month. I had completely forgotten about the book, but now that you ask, I just added up all-time sales for the book. $211 in earnings. I'll take it."

After paying a writer to write one of the worst ideas for a book and failing almost every step along the way, he (by the time you're reading this) made back his costs and will continue to make a tiny bit of profit every month, too.

Understand how powerful time is in this business. It is truly your biggest asset because the more time passes, the more profit every book you publish makes. The first books we published back in 2016 still produce income for us every single month. Three years from now, that failed pi book will have made Alex over $1,000 in earnings, and ten years from now, it'll be much more.

I understand that's nothing to brag about, but it's acceptable for something he didn't put that many hours into. When you do the publishing process right, you can make a lot of money with a few books. For example, Kyle made $29,000 in one month and shared his success story in our private AIA Facebook group with the heading "The Power of Publishing" and three fire emojis.

He said, "I just had my biggest month yet! This business model has been an absolute gamechanger in my life. The freedom it gives you is just incredible and still blows my mind."

And then, on the next line, bold and centered, he wrote: $29,711.12.

"What kept me going the most and gave me the belief it was possible was being a part of communities like this and seeing others post their results like Christian was saying. And I hope my results can inspire others to stick with it like I did when it got hard."

Then he thanked us at the end for "building such a dope community" (see the screenshot below).

Kyle Verrier
Conversation starter · 3 January at 12:07

The Power of Publishing 

I just had my biggest month yet! This business model has been an absolute gamechanger in my life. The freedom it gives you is just incredible and still blows my mind

$29,711.12

I have published 13 books so far, but all very high quality

What kept me going the most and gave me the belief it was possible was being apart of communities like this and seeing others post their results like Christian was saying. And I hope my results can inspire others to stick with it like I did when it got hard.

A huge thanks to Christian and Rasmus for so openly sharing and supporting everything they know, and building such a dope community.

The only way you fail with this is by doing nothing. So just don't do nothing. That's it. If you actually publish just one book/audiobook, you will make money. End of story. The biggest mistake you can make is not having something out and selling, making you money passively every month.

How much you make will depend on how well you do the steps you're about to read in the following chapters.

End-of-Module Roundup

In this module, you learned what the Freedom Shortcut is—it is what we and the thousands of people we've coached have already used to make true passive income. Some have even quit their jobs.

You learned what passive income actually looks like. It is not "getting paid for doing nothing." It's doing something and then getting paid over and over for the work you've already done. You have to build a machine that can make money without you first, then it becomes passive income.

You learned who this book is for and isn't for. It's for anyone that wants more free time and wants to make money without relying on a job for the rest of their life. It's not for those who want to get rich quick or think that making money online is a scam.

You learned why book publishing on Amazon and Audible is such a powerful business model:

- You have Amazon to remove all the complexity that comes with having a business.
- You get to tap into Amazon's massive audience of buyers.
- You can never run out of inventory.
- Books and audiobooks are something you create once and get paid for indefinitely.
- Books can make a significant impact on other people's lives.
- You can make money creating books about topics you love.
- Audiobooks are an exploding market.
- So. Many. Income. Streams.
- It is literally passive income.

You learned the pitfalls of the business model:

- You will not get rich quick.
- You will need to invest money.
- Publishing probably won't make you a millionaire, but it'll make you free.
- Publishing on Audible is only available to people from or in the US, UK, Canada, or Ireland.

You learned what the three main ingredients of a book are:

1) Written Manuscript
2) Book Cover
3) Audio Narration

You learned about Amazon's exploding audiobook platform, Audible. With Audible booming in popularity, it opens up a world of opportunity for people like you and me to profit from audiobooks.

You learned that, at the time of this writing, there are 1,224 physical products on Amazon for every one audiobook for sale on Audible—a fraction of the competition comparatively.

You learned how not to fail—Just follow the steps and actually publish something.

The Audiobook Income Process

Now that you've read this far, I believe you have a strong foundational understanding of the business model, so we're ready to get into the step-by-step how-to.

What I'm about to reveal to you is what we call the Audiobook Income Process and it goes like this:

1) Choose

2) Outsource

3) Launch

4) Multiply

Let's dive into Step 1 of making money with book publishing on Amazon and Audible: Choosing Your Niche.

MODULE 2

CHOOSE

THERE ARE HUNDREDS OF MICRO-NICHES OUT THERE WITH LITTLE COMPETITION AND AN INCREDIBLE OPPORTUNITY FOR PROFIT.

10 NICHE FUNDAMENTALS

The first step to creating passive income with books and audiobooks is deciding what niche your books will be about.

What is a niche?

In general business terms, a niche is a segment of a larger market.

In this instance, the larger market is all book buyers. But there's no way we can create a book that is going to appeal to all book buyers, which is why we need to niche down and create books for a more specific segment of people.

Outside of fiction books, there are approximately 10 main book niches, which I will reveal shortly. But for the sake of this example, let's look at the 4 biggest non-fiction niches:

1) Self-Help

2) Health, Fitness, and Dieting

3) Business and Investing

4) Crafts, Hobbies, and Home

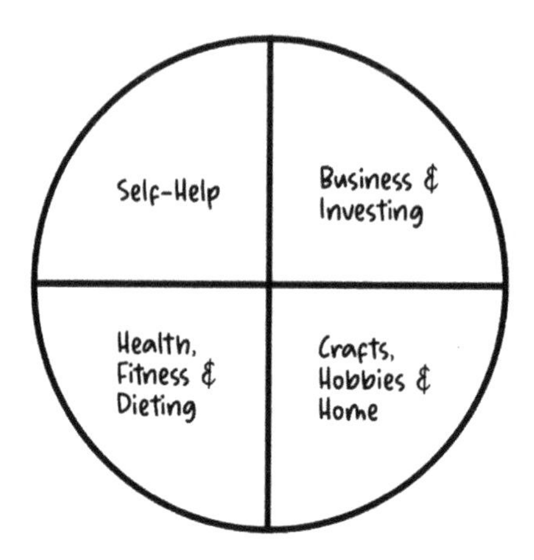

Within a niche, there are sub-niches that target a more specific segment of people. For example:

- Marketing and Sales
- Entrepreneurship
- Personal Finance
- Sustainable Living
- Crafts
- Outdoors
- Alternative Medicine
- Exercise
- Dieting
- Spiritual
- Self-esteem
- Productivity

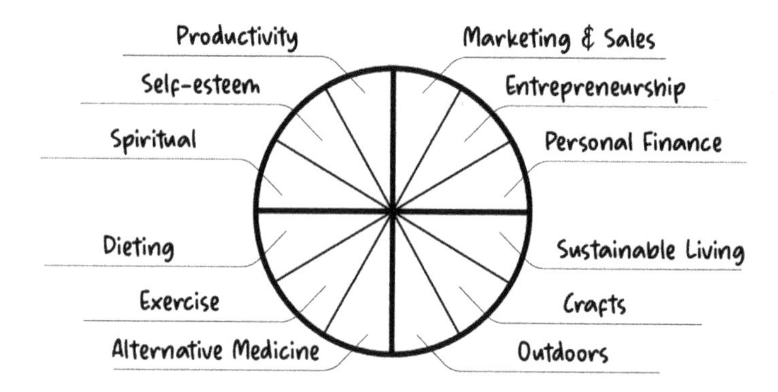

Within a sub-niche, there are even more sub-sub-niches. For example:

- Copywriting
- Persuasion
- Home based
- Consulting
- Retirement planning
- Budgeting
- RV living
- Container gardening
- Quilting
- Soap making
- Survival skills
- Fishing
- Energy healing
- Aromatherapy
- Steady state cardio
- HIIT
- Vegan
- Low carb
- New age spirituality
- Crystals
- Anxiety
- Confidence
- Habits
- Time management

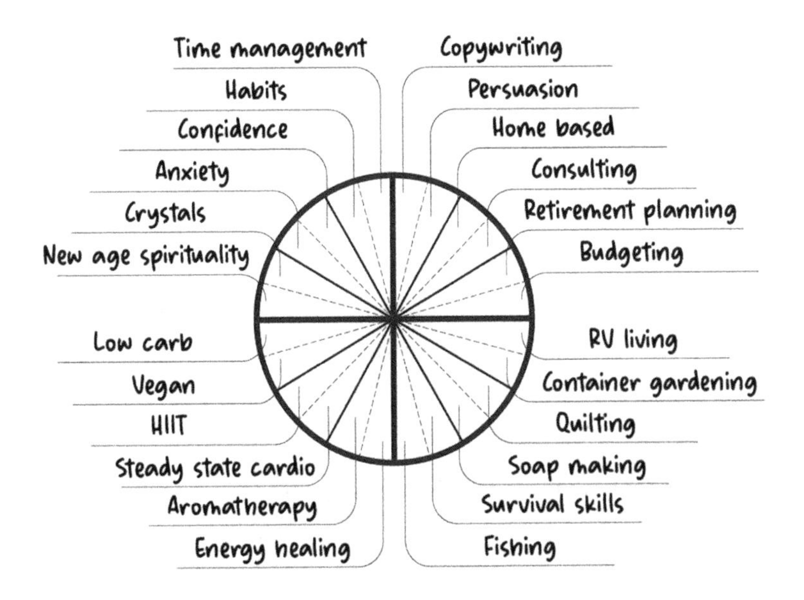

This example is just scratching the surface. No, this is scratching the surface of scratching the surface. These are just 24 examples of topics you could create a book about. There are WAY more sub-niches, sub-sub-niches, and so on to explore here, and these are only 4 of the 10 best niches. There are thousands of topics you could create a book about and dozens of ways to create different books about the same topic.

For example, here are 10 potential books about the same topic—the keto diet—yet they are still unique and provide value in their own way.

1) Keto for Beginners
2) Keto Cookbook
3) Keto Meal Plan
4) 30 Day Keto Cleanse
5) Keto Snacks
6) Keto Desserts
7) Keto Meal Prep
8) Keto for Weight Loss
9) Keto on a Budget
10) Keto for Women

The beauty of niching down is that the more specific you get about the topic of your books, the more your books will stand out to a certain segment of people. Plus, you'll have far fewer competitors.

On the other hand, you might think *I don't want to niche down too much or else the market for my book will be too small.*

While that is possible in rare cases, it's very unlikely. Even the seemingly smallest of sub-sub-niches have hundreds of thousands of potential buyers.

One of the first mistakes I see beginners make is not niching down enough. If you create a general book about weight loss for ANYONE who wants to lose weight, that's not going to garner interest because they've already seen it a million times before.

You need to be more specific. For example:

- People have preferences as to HOW they want to lose weight. Some people want to use fasting, or count calories, or do HIIT workouts, or go on the keto diet.
- WHY do they want to lose weight? Some people want to get a six-pack, some want to lose 50 pounds, some want to be healthier and live longer.
- WHO is this book for? A 25-year-old man and a 65-year-old woman do not want the same kind of weight loss book.

These are all examples of how you can niche down in the weight loss niche. These details about your book will be communicated in the title, on the cover, in the book description, and inside the book.

> "If you chase two rabbits,
> you will not catch either one."
>
> —Russian Proverb

What that quote means is—If you try to make a book that appeals to everyone, you will end up with a book that appeals to no one.

Nonfiction or Fiction?

This is a question that oftens comes up. Nonfiction is based on facts and real life, such as the one you're reading right now. Fiction books are about madeup events and stories.

We only publish nonfiction books and here's why:

Costs: The longer the book, the more expensive it is to get written. Full-length fiction books are often 50,000 to 100,000 or more words. For nonfiction, around 25,000 to 30,000 words is generally the sweet spot.

Buying habits: Fiction readers prefer to buy ebooks and usually they'll be priced at $0.99 which means you have to sell a lot of copies to see significant income. Most nonfiction readers buy print books and audiobooks, so you don't have to sell as many copies as with fiction.

Value: Fiction is entertainment. People love to be entertained, but it doesn't have the potential to be life-transformational. Nonfiction is education, which people will pay much more money for.

Passive income: Fiction is not as passive because it relies heavily on email marketing and cross-promotions. With nonfiction, most sales will come from people searching for a topic on Amazon/Audible, and then finding your book that way.

Potential to sell more than just books: Because nonfiction is educational, there are a lot of opportunities to sell much more than just books to your audience. For example, online courses, coaching, services, and affiliate products. With fiction, there's almost nothing else you can sell other than more books.

Beginner-friendly: There are no barriers to getting started in nonfiction because, contrary to popular belief, you do ***not*** need to be famous or have an audience. The success of beginner publishers is enough proof of that, but I break it down and explain why in Chapter 14. This means anyone can get started in nonfiction and find success faster than with fiction.

To summarize, nonfiction is:

1) Low cost

2) Actually passive

3) Easy for beginners

It's not because you can't make good money selling fiction books, it's just harder—in my humble opinion.

Now before you start brainstorming and writing down as many niche ideas as you can think of, let me make it easy for you.

The best way to start is by exploring the 20 different nonfiction book categories listed on the Amazon book store. Amazon calls it "categories." Some people call it "genres." We call it "niches." It's the same thing, just different terminology.

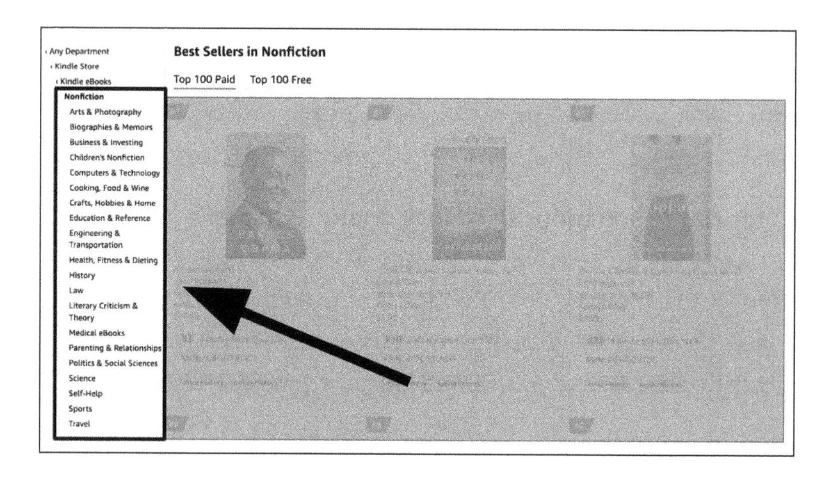

From my years of experience and having published books in most of these categories, I can already tell you which ones are the best and worst to choose from. There are ten categories you should eliminate right off the bat because they are either too technical or just a bit tricky for various reasons.

1) Biographies & memoirs
2) Children's nonfiction
3) Education & reference
4) Engineering & transportation
5) History
6) Law
7) Literary criticism & theory
8) Medical ebooks
9) Politics & Social Sciences
10) Science

That leaves us with:

1) Arts & Photography
2) Business & Investing
3) Computers & Technology
4) Cooking, Food, & Wine
5) Crafts, Hobbies, & Home
6) Health, Fitness, & Dieting
7) Parenting & Relationships
8) Self-Help
9) Sports & Outdoors
10) Travel

Within each of these categories, there are 10, 50, sometimes 100+ different niches. If you go on Amazon and click on the category, it will open another menu of sub-categories (or sub-niches, same thing). Go ahead and explore these categories and subcategories just to get some ideas flowing.

To help, I'll give three examples of random—but highly profitable—sub-niches within each category.

1) Arts & Photography—Drawing, Crochet, Photography
2) Business & Investing—Investing, Marketing & Sales, Job Hunting
3) Computers & Technology—Computer Programming, Web Design, App Development
4) Cooking, Food, & Wine—Budget Cooking, Vegan Cooking, Juicing & Smoothies

5) Crafts, Hobbies, & Home—Woodworking, Guitar, Soap Making
6) Health, Fitness, & Dieting—Home Workouts, Keto Diet, Addiction
7) Parenting & Relationships—Dating for Men, Parenting, Marriage Counseling
8) Self-Help—Memory Improvement, Stress Management, Personal Growth
9) Sports & Outdoors—Tennis, Golf, Fishing
10) Travel—Travel Guides, RV Living, Camping

How do I know these niches are profitable? Because there are many books in each of these niches published by the Average Joe (like you and me) that make $1,000+ per month per book. The 30 examples I listed are literally less than 1% of all the different niches you could publish books about.

One of the biggest mistakes I see people make is shying away from certain niches because they have some preconceived notions of them. You may see a niche and think, *There's very little demand, no one buys books about this topic.* But you could very easily be wrong. Let me give you an example.

A student of ours has a book that sells hundreds of copies and makes thousands of dollars every month.

If you were to go on Facebook and search for groups about this topic, you would find dozens of groups with thousands of members in them. One Facebook group even has over 40,000 members in it!

You might expect this topic to be something we all know is

popular such as self-help, weight loss, or marketing ... but no. What is his book about?

The Rubik's Cube.

He makes full-time income just from publishing simple guide books about how to solve a Rubik's Cube. It may seem like a small niche in the grand scheme, but there are literally millions of people in the world who want to learn how to solve a Rubik's Cube.

So just because a niche appears small doesn't mean it is. Do your research first. There are hundreds of micro-niches out there with little competition and an incredible opportunity for profit.

STAY FOCUSED ON ONE MISSION WITH A SINGLE AIM AND GOAL RATHER THAN GIVING EFFORT IN MANY DIFFERENT DIRECTIONS ALL AT ONCE.

11 THE ART OF ONE

Here is one of the best pieces of advice I can give you that I wish someone had told me years ago when I first got started. *Stick to one niche*. Yes, you will get results even if you publish books about all different topics, but they will be a fraction of what you'll achieve by focusing on just one niche.

If you're publishing books about all kinds of topics, then you're being very inefficient with your time, energy, and focus. Imagine you get one watering can full of water every day. This represents all the energy you have to put into your publishing business.

You can choose to spread this finite amount of water among five plants, giving them just enough to survive. Or you can dedicate the entire can of water to one plant, giving it all the nutrients it needs to eventually grow into a large, beautiful tree.

Stay focused on one mission with a single aim and goal rather than giving effort in many different directions all at once. Focus on publishing books in just one niche, and you'll know that niche inside and out. You'll understand exactly what kind of problems your customers have, and the exact kind of books they want. Do not spread your efforts thin by putting 20% of your effort among five different niches.

What's also important to know is that there is not just one niche that is right for you. There are 100+ niches that are right for you. Some may be better than others, but there are 100+ that will give you life-changing results. The key is to pick one that you can commit to 100%.

12 THE SCIENCE OF THE GAME

The game of business and making money is just as much an art as it is a science. That means business is driven by facts, data, and analytics, but it is also intuitive and abstract. When it comes to picking your niche, it's essential to look at what the data tells us, but it's also just as important to consider your liking for that niche.

This chapter will show you how to use data and numbers to determine a niche's profitability. To do so, we need to measure the levels of demand and competition within a niche. Amazon makes this very easy for us because they provide all the data we need.

When it comes to demand, we want it to be as high as possible. We want a lot of people already buying books about this topic.

With competition, we want it as low as possible. We want few people already selling books about this topic.

The most profitable niches will be ones with high demand (lots of people buying books) and low competition (few people selling books), BUT it's not a requirement to have both. A niche with higher competition can still be very profitable, but then it better have high demand as well. A niche with lower demand can still be very profitable, but then it better also have low competition. It's about finding a balance.

The way you determine the demand within a niche is by measuring how well books about that topic already sell. We can measure how much any book on Amazon sells by looking at its Best Sellers Rank (BSR). Here is how Amazon defines BSR on their customer help page:

> *"The Amazon Best Sellers Rank (BSR) is calculated based on Amazon sales and is updated hourly to reflect recent and historical sales of every item sold on Amazon."*

A book with a BSR of 1 means it is the #1 best-selling book on all of Amazon and literally sells 10,000+ copies every day. Whoever owns that book is making millions and millions of dollars every month.

BSR #1 = #1 best selling book on Amazon

BSR #10,000 = 10,000th best selling book on Amazon (roughly 400 sales per month)

BSR #100,000 = 100,000th best selling book on Amazon (roughly 50 sales per month)

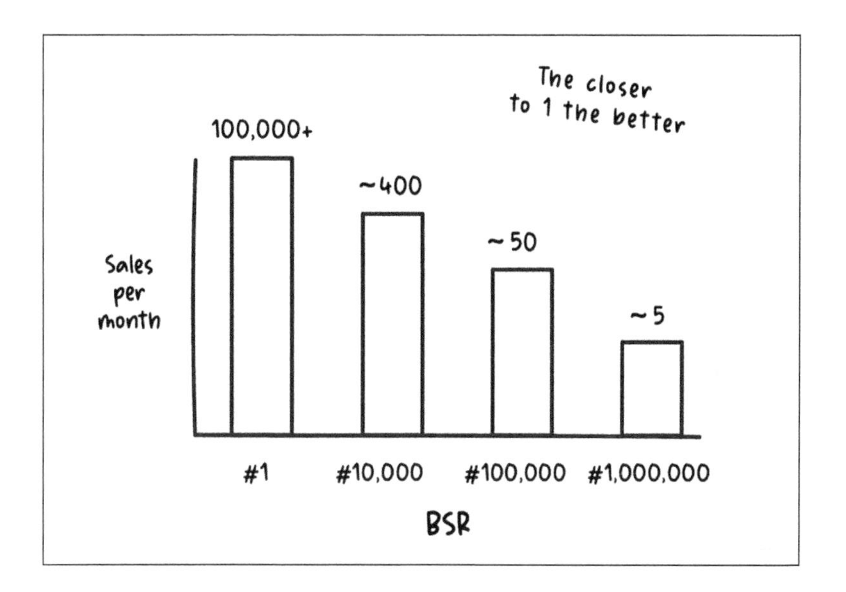

If we go to the Best Sellers List on Amazon, we can see exactly what type of books are selling well. The Best Sellers List is simply a list of all the top selling books which can be filtered by category (niche) and sub-category (sub-niche).

Every book on Amazon has a BSR, so we can see what types of books are selling well.

Here are five books from Amazon with their BSR shown.

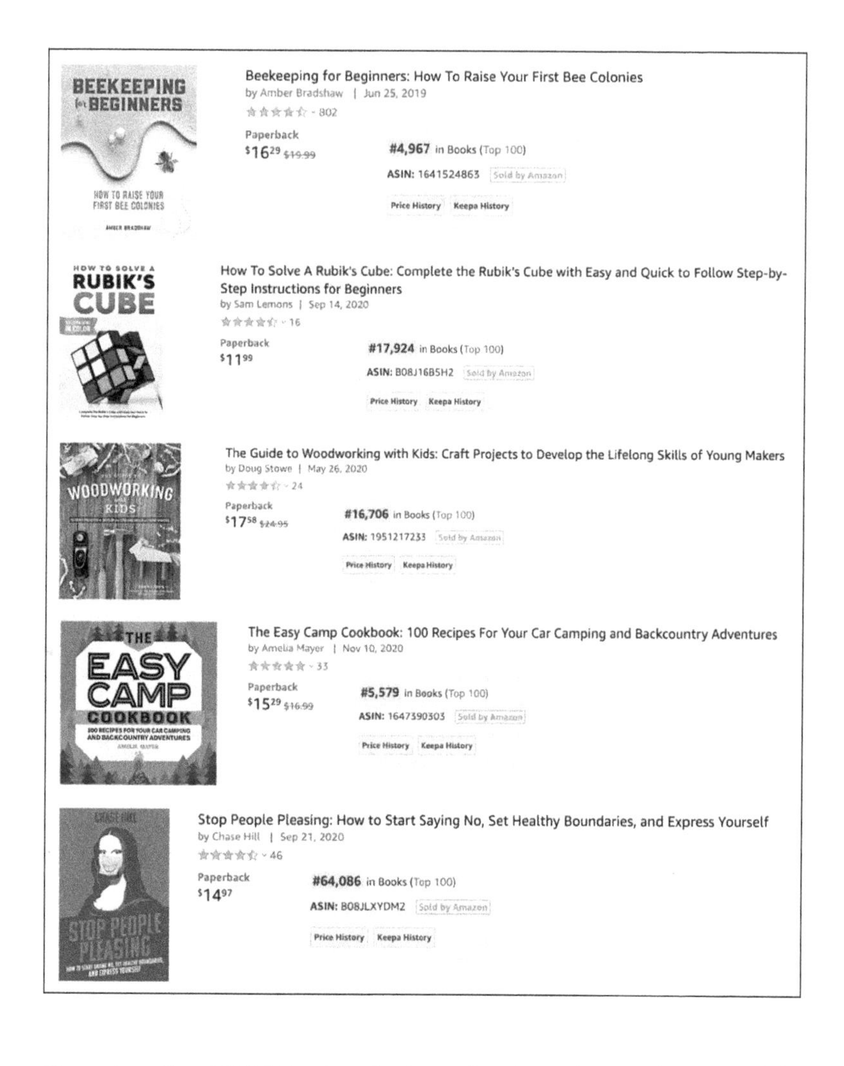

Based on the BSR,* the book about beekeeping makes roughly 600–700 print book sales per month ($3000+ per month).

The book about how to solve a Rubik's Cube makes about 200–250 print book sales per month ($1,000+ per month).

The book about woodworking for kids makes about 200–250 print book sales per month ($1,500+ per month).

The book about camping recipes makes about 600–700 print book sales per month ($3,000+ per month).

The book about how to stop people pleasing makes about 70–100 print book sales per month ($600+ per month).

*Sales calculated using the Amazon Book Sales Calculator from tckpublishing.com.

These are examples of singular books that are bringing in consistent, life-changing income every month. Even if one book could bring in just $200 passively every month, would that make a difference in your life? That's a car payment taken care of every month from just one book. And that money comes in month after month, year after year.

I hope you're starting to see how Amazon publishing works and why it has completely changed our lives.

Remember that for each book you publish, you are selling it in three formats—ebook, print book, and audiobook. The sales numbers I shared from those five books are JUST the print book sales. This does NOT include the ebook and audiobook sales. Each book will have 3 BSRs—one for each format.

So if a book has a BSR of 100,000, it means it's making about 50 sales per month *in just one format*. Add up the total sales of all three, and you have the book's total earnings for one month.

Now that you understand how BSR works, how do we use this data to determine demand?

We determine demand by searching the topic in Amazon and counting how many books on page 1 of the Amazon search results have a BSR of 30,000 or below.

Why do we do it this way?

If a book has a BSR of 30,000 or below, then that book is generating at least $1,000 per month. If there are already books on this topic making at least $1,000 per month, then we know the potential is already there for you to do it too.

How many books should have a BSR under 30,000?

There isn't a cut and dry correct answer to this question, but we like to see at least three books with a BSR of 30,000 or less. That tells us the demand is there. The more books with a BSR of less than 30,000, the better.

Because it's tough to explain how to do this in a book, I've recorded a bonus video training where I walk through this step-by-step and show you how to determine any niche's profitability. To watch this video training, go to publishinglife.com/niche.

Please take the time to watch the bonus video training because it will make everything covered in this chapter a lot clearer!

Now, moving onto the other side of the equation: competition. We need to measure the competition and see how easy it would be to come in and compete with other books in our niche.

Competition is broken up into two parts:

1) number of competitors and

2) strength of competitors.

Number of Competitors

Here we're looking to see how many other books we would be competing against in a niche. To do so, we look at how many other books on this topic are already published.

This is extremely straightforward because all you do is search for your niche in Audible and look at the number of search results that appear.

We do this search on Audible instead of Amazon because we want to be sure we're looking at data from Audible and not just Amazon. Audiobook sales are at least as important as print book and ebook sales, if not more important. So we want to be sure we're looking at both platforms.

Whether you're looking at Amazon or Audible, there is a very strong correlation between the two. So if there is high demand on Amazon, there is most likely high demand on Audible. If there is low competition on Audible, there is most likely low competition on Amazon.

Here are the general guidelines for determining competition based on Audible search results:

Fewer than 100 search results is very low on the competitive scale, 100 to 299 search results is low, 300 to 499 is medium, and 500 or more search results is high.

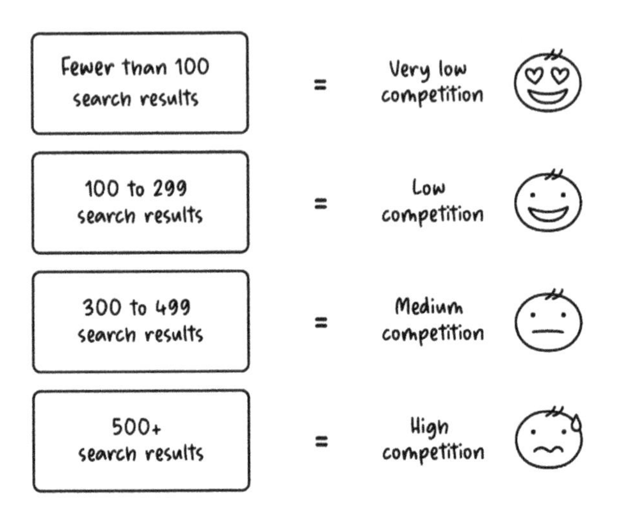

For this example, let's use the home workouts niche. When we type "home workouts" into the Audible search bar, there are 66 search results that appear. So on Audible, home workouts has very little competition.

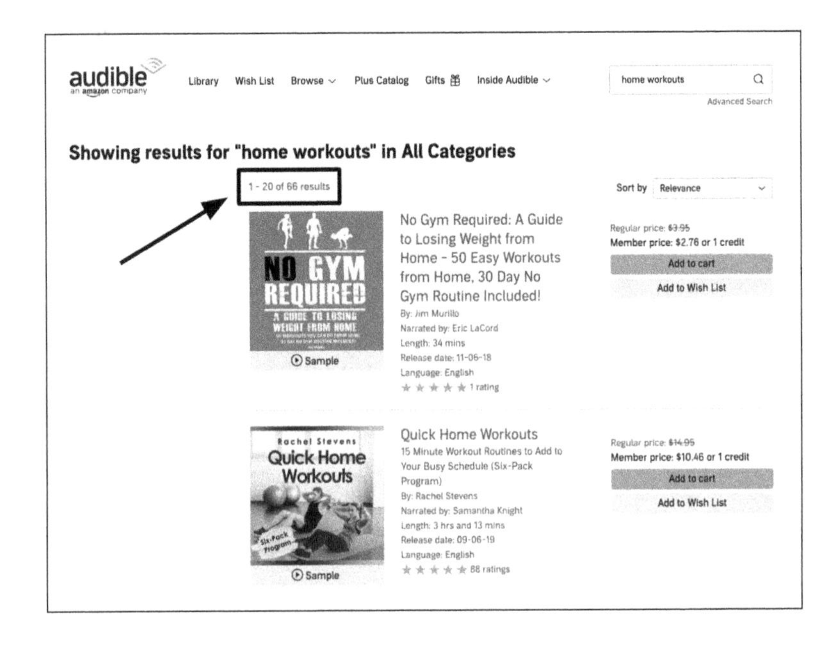

(All numbers are taken from the time of writing this book, so they will have changed by the time you are reading this.)

Strength of Competitors

Strength of competitors is the other half of the competition equation, and equally as important as the number of competitors.

If you see two niches both have 50 books published in them, that does NOT mean that the level of competition in those niches is equal—because not all competition is created equally.

If the one niche consists of 50 lower-quality books, all with fewer than 10 reviews, that would be very weak competition. If the other niche consists of 50 higher-quality books, all with 1,000+ reviews, that would be very strong competition.

So to determine the strength of the competition within a niche, the key indicator we're looking at is reviews. How many reviews do your competitors' books have?

If you go into a niche like self-help, you're competing against the fiercest competition there is ... juggernauts like Tony Robbins, Jordan Peterson, Tim Ferriss, Robert Kiyosaki, James Clear, Dale Carnegie, etc.

If someone is faced with the decision to buy your book with 10 reviews or Tony Robbins' book with 10,000 reviews, which one do you think they'll pick? Unless it's their mom (let's be honest, *even if it is their mom*), 9 times out of 10, Tony is winning that battle.

On the other hand, let's look at home workouts again. On the first page of Audible search results, this is what the number of reviews per book looks like:

Reviews	Books
0 - 10	12
10 - 30	2
30 - 50	2
50 - 100	2
100 - 200	1
200 - 500	0
500 - 1000	1
1000+	0

In the home workouts niche, there is only one "strong" competitor. The vast majority of the books here have fewer than 10 reviews, so the competition is far from fierce. In fact, it's incredibly weak.

As a rule of thumb, if you have a niche where more than 5 books have 500+ reviews, then the competition is looking pretty stiff.

Steer clear of niches where you have some big name authority books and authors because most readers will gravitate toward their books instead of yours. You can still make good money in those niches, but you can absolutely dominate if there are no authority figures present in your niche.

Using this strategy for determining demand and competition, you can quickly run some numbers to find out if a niche is profitable or not. The best niches are the ones with a balance between high demand and low competition, so be sure to weigh both factors evenly. And a final reminder to not prejudge any niche before looking at the data. Numbers don't lie.

13 THE ART OF THE GAME

In the documentary called *Michael Jordan to the Max,* Michael Jordan was asked, "What's the secret to being the best basketball player in the world?"

His answer: "The secret is to fall in love with the game."[5]

What he meant is that when you really love the game, then you don't need to force yourself to get to work—you'll just do it because it's what you want to do more than anything else. If you don't love the game, then it becomes a chore, and it starts to feel like hard work. All you have at that point is motivation and ambition to drive you into action, and those feelings aren't always there. They come and go.

So the second half of the equation when deciding which niche to go into is choosing something you will have fun with! Neither I nor any set of data can say what that is for you.

---

5 *Michael Jordan to the Max,* directed by Don Kempf and James D. Stern, written by Jonathan Hock. (2000) IMAX Documentary Film.

There can be a highly profitable niche that's a great choice for one person, but not suitable for someone else. That's because if you have to force yourself to do the work, then it's much less likely to get done. But as long as you do the work, and you get books and audiobooks published on Amazon and Audible, then you will make passive income. But if you can't bring yourself to take the necessary actions, you'll never make a penny.

Answering the question "What am I passionate about?" isn't always so easy. I prefer to think of it in a different way. Rather, ask yourself, "What could I talk about all day for free and be very happy doing it?"

In my opinion, this is a better way of figuring out what you really enjoy. Off the top of my head, here are ten things I could talk about all day without getting bored:

- Travel
- Food
- Online business
- Basketball
- Football
- Fantasy sports
- Powerlifting
- Bodybuilding
- Pokemon
- Bali

If I were new to publishing and just getting started, my niche would be within one of those ten topics. I would look at the demand and competition numbers like I showed in the last chapter to make my final choice.

Whatever niche you choose doesn't have to be at the top of your list. It doesn't have to be your absolute favorite thing in the world, but you really should have some sort of personal connection to that niche. When you're reading your book, you shouldn't be bored about the information inside or feel like you're forcing yourself to read it. If you're running a business around something you don't care about, chances are you will never see it through to the end.

Patrick Jackson even talks about this in the case study interview (publishinglife.com/patrick) where he says, "I love this business. As soon as I wake up in the morning, I can't wait to get to my computer." He had a passion for learning foreign languages even though he wasn't good at it, and he turned that into a life-changing passive income machine.

Getting paid way above the average salary to do something you love and be your own boss with the freedom to do whatever you like ... What more could you ever ask for in a career?

When choosing your niche, remember to pick something that 1) you're passionate about and 2) passes the profitability test. That's your sweet spot.

Making money is so much more fun when you're doing something you enjoy. So choose something you enjoy.

> "If you love what you do, you'll never work a day in your life."
>
> —Marc Anthony

14 "BUT ... I'M A NOBODY."

People are always looking for all the reasons why they can NOT succeed. One of the most common reasons I hear from people as to why they can't make money publishing books and audiobooks is, "I'm not famous, no one would buy a book from me."

It's a valid thought to have as it's true that many published authors are indeed famous. But have you ever thought about how they became famous?

The reason why people like Robert Kiyosaki, Tim Ferriss, Napoleon Hill, Stephen Covey, James Clear, and many others are famous is because they wrote a good book!

People buy books because they are looking for a solution to a problem. If you have the solution, they don't care who you are. Did you buy this book because I'm "famous"? No, you bought it because you want to create freedom in your life by making passive income online, and I have the solution for that. You honestly couldn't care one bit whether I'm famous or not.

That's exactly how all other readers feel as well. If they see a book that can help them solve a Rubik's Cube, learn how to invest in the stock market, learn a new language, whatever it is, that is 100 times more important to them than the name on the front cover.

You might be thinking, *I would never buy a book from a no name author.* That's great, but with all due respect, what you would or wouldn't do doesn't matter. That is not a reflection of typical buyer behavior. The data shows that most people have no problem buying books by "no name" authors. All of our students publish under a pen name or under their own name. Either way, they are all "no names" and collectively they've sold millions of book copies.

Now that we're on the topic of pen names ... A pen name (also known as a pseudonym) is a made-up name that is listed as the author of the book. It can be a first and last name or it can even be a brand name, such as Mindful Meditation Club if you want to publish books about meditation. Either way, the pen name you choose will not play a role in the success of your books. It's just a name.

Pen names are a very common practice and are usually used to protect the author's identity. That's why we teach our students to use a pen name.

The biggest authors in the world use pen names too. Have you ever heard of Robert Galbraith? Well, that's a pen name J.K. Rowling (author of the Harry Potter books) uses to write and sell books in the crime fiction niche.

None of Patrick Jackson's readers had a clue who he was when they first purchased his books, but based on the title and book cover, it was clear that his books could help them. In the case study interview with Patrick, he says:

> *"I wouldn't consider myself an expert at learning Spanish or any other language, and that actually helps because I'm coming from the viewpoint as someone that's learning. So I'm on the same journey as them. I'm just a little bit further ahead than they are on that journey."*

I feel confident saying that you have probably learned something from someone else who wasn't the best at that thing. But you were still able to get a lot of value from that person, right? Because they knew more than you, and that was enough.

Remember, you're not writing your book! A professional writer is. They will like to have some guidance from you (after all, it is your book), but they don't need an expert to give them all the content. That is their job. Your writer will have some level of experience in your niche, or they might even be an expert themselves.

It sucks seeing people not publish books and audiobooks on Amazon just because they think they're not qualified for it—as if they need some sort of degree or certificate to get permission. The question is: *Can you publish a book that will help someone in any way?* Good, then do it. You don't need permission.

End-of-Module Roundup

In this module, you learned what a niche is, why it's important to choose only one niche, and the best way to choose your niche.

You learned the two factors you need to consider when picking your niche. They are:

1) Demand & Competition: How many books have a BSR under 30,000, and how many other books are you competing against?

2) Your Passion for the Niche: Is it a topic you would enjoy doing, or would it feel more like a chore?

You learned what BSR is and how to use it to determine demand.

You learned how to use the Amazon and Audible search results to determine competition.

You learned how to differentiate weak competition from strong competition.

You learned not to prejudge any niche because you will be shocked what kind of books in "small" niches actually sell really well.

You learned to focus your efforts within one niche rather than spreading yourself thin.

You learned that each book creates three separate income streams as an ebook, print book, and audiobook.

You learned book buyers only care about getting a solution to their problem and that not being famous or an expert is nothing but an excuse to never get started.

Now, let's move on to the next module: How to create your book, step-by-step.

MODULE 3

OUTSOURCE

EVEN IF YOU ARE A WRITER YOURSELF, YOUR TIME IS STILL BETTER SPENT GETTING SOMEONE ELSE TO WRITE FOR YOU.

15

THE JAMES PATTERSON MODEL

If you're an avid reader of fiction books, chances are you probably know who James Patterson is. But if you're anything like me, then you're not much of a reader, and you have no idea who he is. Well, James Patterson has published over 500 books, sold over 400 million copies, and has a net worth of over $800 million. He is the most successful "author" of all time.

I put "author" in quotations because while he is the one credited with writing his books and the one being paid the majority of the money from his book sales, he is technically not the sole writer of his books.

He works with ghostwriters to help write his books for him.

So what is ghostwriting exactly?

Ghostwriter

[gōst-rīt-er] *noun*

A person whose job it is to write material for someone else who is named the author.

Ghostwriting is one of the most common practices in the book publishing industry. You may or may not know that Michelle Obama's book *Becoming*, which is one of the best-selling books of all time, was written by a ghostwriter. David Goggins' hit book *Can't Hurt Me* was written by a ghostwriter. When you see a celebrity release a book, it's often ghostwritten. Hundreds and hundreds of world-famous books were written by ghostwriters, including a large portion of James Patterson's 500+ book catalog.

The reason why it's so widely done is because it just makes sense. You have someone such as yourself with the desire to publish a book, but you don't have the skills or time to write it. Then you have someone else, a writer, who is very skilled at writing and loves doing it.

In a perfect world, writers would just write all day and get paid for it. They don't want to deal with the book cover design, launching the book, getting reviews, or any of that. They just want to write.

That's why it's a match made in heaven when a publisher, like you and me, can work together with a ghostwriter to create books. We get a book we can publish and make money from, and the writer gets to write while being paid upfront for their work without having to deal with all the other stuff they hate.

It's a win-win.

The role you have in your Amazon publishing business is the same role James Patterson has in his $800 million publishing empire. He's the manager, the chef, the CEO, whatever you want to call it, but he is NOT the writer, NOT the cover designer, and NOT the narrator. He helps by coming up with the ideas for the books with a book outline, coming up with the titles, and just kickstarting the entire process.

Using this model, James Patterson can release more than 30 full-length books every year as opposed to most authors who write themselves and usually publish just one to two books a year at best. This is why I say that even if you are a writer yourself, your time is still better spent getting someone else to write for you.

It takes a lot of experience and management to publish 30 great books a year, so if you're wondering how many books a year you should publish, it's this: As many as you can handle without the quality of your books suffering. If that's one to two books a month, great. If it's one to two books every six months, that's great too.

Another comment we often get when we explain how ghost-writing works is "that must be expensive." Well, it can be. Famous high-end ghostwriters charge tens to hundreds of thousands of dollars because they know how valuable their work is.

These are not the writers we use. We use a strategy that we like to call Low-Cost Expert Outsourcing.

This doesn't only apply to ghostwriting. We use it for all steps in the book creation process, like book cover design and audio-book narration too.

With the growth of the internet, thousands of writers have swarmed to freelance websites like Upwork.com to offer their services, and many companies specializing in ghostwriting have also been started.

Here you can find super talented writers for pennies on the dollar as they're just starting their writing careers and looking to build a portfolio. This is how we get impressive full-length books written for just $500–$800. More on this soon.

16 CRAFTING YOUR TITLE

Before you get a writer for your book, or even before you create your book outline, the very first step is to create your book title.

We do this first because your book title is paramount to the success of your book. If you create your outline first, you're pigeonholing yourself into making your book title fit your outline. You want complete freedom to create the best book title you can, then create an outline to fit your title.

There are two key purposes your book title serves: To get seen and get sold.

1. Get seen

Your book title tells Amazon and Audible when and where to show your book in their search results. If your book title does not include the keywords people are searching in the Amazon search bar, then it will not be shown in the Amazon search results.

When someone searches a keyword into Amazon/Audible that is related to the topic of your book, you want your book to show up. The only way that can happen is if your title contains those keywords that Amazon's customers are searching for..

Keyword

[kē-wərd] *noun*

A word or phrase that a customer searches in order to find a specific product.

Whenever someone tells me their book title and asks for feedback, my first question is always, "What are people searching on Amazon and Audible to find your book?" If the words they tell me are not in the title, I tell them to rewrite it.

Figuring out which words you need to include in your title is simple. You go to Amazon and Audible, you search for the main keywords related to your book, and then see which suggested search terms show up.

For the sake of this example, let's say you wanted to create a book about smoothie recipes. If you type in "smoothies" in the Amazon search bar, here are the suggested search results you would get: smoothies for weight loss, smoothies recipe book, smoothies for diabetics, smoothies for health, smoothies recipes, smoothies and juices, smoothies for beginners, smoothies for kids.

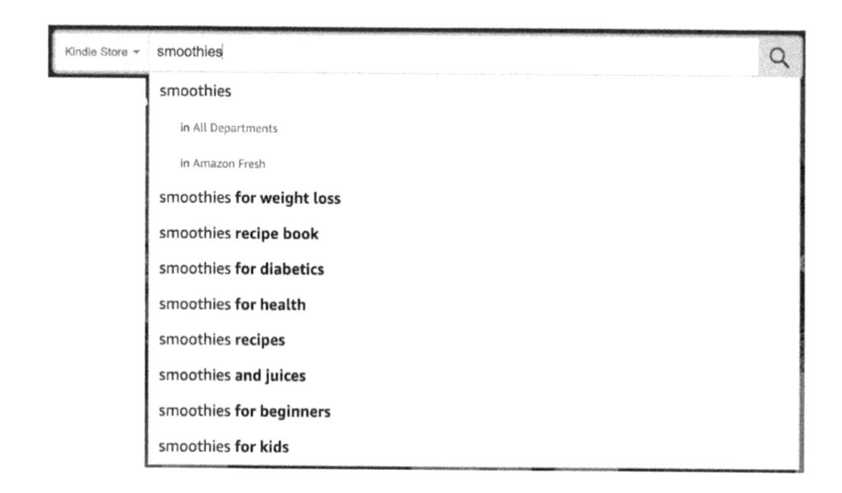

We then extract all the suggested search terms: for weight loss, recipe book, for diabetics, for health, recipes, and juices, for beginners, for kids.

Now let's boil that down into single words: smoothies, juices, weight loss, health, recipes, diabetics, beginners, kids.

These are the words you want to put into your title. You won't get all of them in, but get in as many as you can without "keyword-stuffing" the title with so many keywords that it becomes ugly.

You can see now why you want to create your book title first before your book outline. If you had your outline or entire book done first, then the content of the book may not match the title you want.

The outline is dictated by the title, not the other way around! Now onto the other purpose of your title...

2. Get sold

Now we need to take the list of keywords we have and fit them into a title in a nice way that compels people to buy our book.

An important question to ask yourself here is, "What goal does someone want to achieve when they buy my book?"

This is where some customer research will be very helpful. This is another reason why you should choose a topic you're passionate about because you'll likely already know it without having to do any research. From the brief smoothie research we did, we saw that one goal people want to achieve is weight loss. On top of that, they obviously also want to make smoothies that taste good.

Knowing all of this, here is a great title for a book about smoothies:

Delicious Smoothies & Juices for Weight Loss: 101 Easy & Healthy Low-Calorie Recipes You Can Make at Home

The keywords I included were smoothies, juices, weight loss, health, and recipes. I left out diabetics, kids, and beginners because the title became ugly when I tried to get those words in. It's about finding a balance.

I used descriptive words like "delicious," "easy," and "low calorie" because I know that's what people want a smoothie to be. I said, "recipes you can make at home," because I know people want it to be easy and done from home.

Now there is also complete clarity as to what this book is about. Someone should be able to read the title and know exactly what they will learn from the book.

This book would also appear in the search rankings because it includes the exact words people are searching on Amazon and Audible.

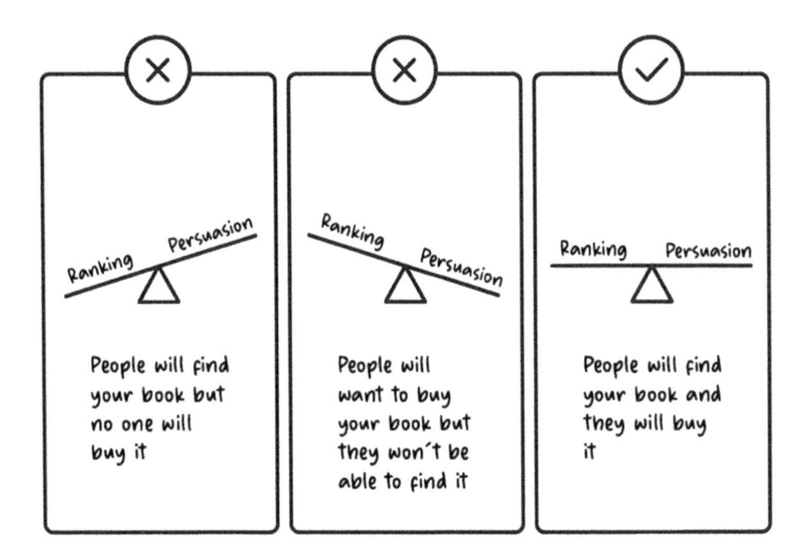

You want to be sure your title has enough keywords in it, but without it being too many and "keyword-stuffed". Not enough keywords and your book won't show up much in the search results. Too many keywords and your title will sound ugly and unprofessional. You need a balanced title that sounds compelling and natural and contains the most important keywords.

So how many keywords should your title include? Anywhere between 2 and 5.

Creating your book title is a rather simple and straightforward process. It starts with assembling a list of keywords people are already using to search on Amazon and Audible, and then making the title sell the book by talking about the goals they want to achieve. Remember, your book is a solution to a problem they are facing.

Your book title doesn't have to be final before moving on to the next step, but it should be 80 percent there.

17

THE QUALITY FEEDBACK LOOP

Now, we're onto the big, scary part of the whole publishing process. Actually creating the book.

Without knowing anything, most people believe they don't have the ability to create an impressive, professional, full-length book—one that could fit in nicely on a bookshelf beside a *New York Times* bestseller. I'm not saying this part is easy, but I am saying it is much easier than you think, and it's doable by anyone, no matter your experience or skill level.

Yes, hard work is involved, but your writer will do the majority of that hard work. Plus, always remember that nothing worth having comes easy. That should be taken literally. If you want easy, then making money and being successful isn't for you. Easy work will never produce anything meaningful and life-changing.

I'm sure it's obvious that one of the most important aspects of a successful book publishing business is having high-quality, valuable books that actually help people. But why is it so important?

Let's walk through a hypothetical situation where we have two books with the exact same title, cover, book description, and narrator. The only difference is the content—the words inside the book. One book (let's call it a bad book) is dull to read, it's repetitive, full of fluff, seems like it was written by a non-native writer, and is just overall not a helpful book. The other book (let's call it a good book) tells compelling stories, is engaging, detailed, to the point, and focused on helping the reader achieve their desired outcome.

If you were to launch both books in the exact same way, the first month of sales would actually look very similar because, from the outside, the two books look the same. But over the course of the following months, you'll see these two books go down very different paths.

A bad book may have had 100 people buy the book, and about half of them will actually sit down, start reading or listening to it, and really give the book a chance. A few chapters in, you'll see the majority of those readers give up on the book and move on with their lives, or they'll be so upset that this book was a waste of time and money and go straight to Amazon or Audible to leave a negative 1-star review.

Then they'll add your author name to a mental list of authors to NEVER buy a book from again, and at the next family gathering, they'll be sure to tell everyone at dinner how disappointing the book was.

On the other hand, a good book will also have 100 people buy the book, and about half of them will actually sit down, start reading or listening to it, and really give the book a chance. A few chapters in, most readers will be focused, engaged, and perhaps even taking notes on their phone about all the best takeaways they don't want to forget (that's what I do at least).

Once they finish the book, they're left feeling educated and optimistic about their own future within that topic. They'll get some email reminders from Amazon and Audible asking for them to leave a positive 5-star review which is the least they could do for the author after giving them such a great experience.

While they're already on Amazon, they'll go check out your author page and see what other books you have for sale. If you have more books about a similar topic, they'll eagerly buy them too. If you have an email list to sign up for, they will happily join that and recommend the book (and you as an author) to everyone at the next family gathering.

Over time, this sets off a feedback loop either in a positive or negative direction. A bad book will gather negative reviews, which leads to fewer sales, which makes your book drop in the Amazon search rankings, which leads to even fewer sales, which makes your book drop even further down the rankings, and so on.

A good book will gather positive reviews, which leads to more sales, which will boost your book up the rankings, which will turn into even more sales and more positive reviews and happy customers buying your other books, which will cause all of your books to rise up the rankings, which will result in more sales, and so on.

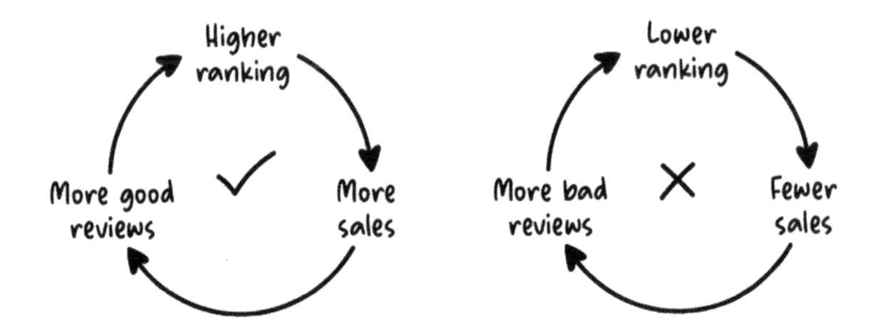

Then, 12 months down the line, you either have a book with poor reviews (the equivalent of putting a big fat DO NOT BUY stamp on the cover), or you literally have an unstoppable money-making machine that pays you hefty sums month after month after month for years and years without you needing to do any additional work.

To further prove my point, here is a post by Juan from inside our private AIA Facebook group:

Here's a little example of two books that I published back in 2015. Five years later, still bring a decent amount of royalties every month. If you're new to publishing, I'm sharing this just to give you guys some perspective. Don't strive to get rich quick with this business model. Think long-term and you'll be thanking yourself 5, 10, 15 years from now that you took action!

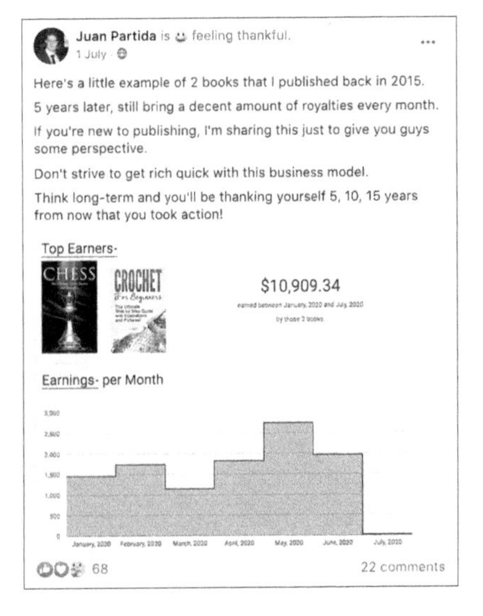

Juan made an extra $10,909 in six months from two books that he published over five years ago. And that money will keep coming in for many, many years because his books are actually helpful to the readers and worthy of 5-star reviews.

A GOOD BOOK WILL SAVE SOMEONE HUNDREDS OF HOURS SCAVENGING THROUGH THE INTERNET TRYING TO PUT THE PIECES TOGETHER THEMSELF.

18 CREATING YOUR OUTLINE

So how do you create books that are 5-star quality? By creating a rock solid book outline.

Creating a great book outline does NOT require prior experience, it does NOT require expertise on a topic, and it does NOT require writing skills in any fashion (if your English is coherent, you're good). It is your writer's job to write a good book. It is only your job to provide them with a roadmap for the content of the book. This just requires some hours of quiet and a few cups of coffee.

When writing your book outline, the first thing you need to understand is that your book should *not* be new information. In today's day and age, there's barely such a thing as new information. Almost all new books are readily available information that is explained in a new way, assembled as an easy-to-follow method, or written for a certain audience.

Your job is to take the good information on your topic that is scattered on the internet, in YouTube videos, perhaps in other books, and organize it in a book that's easy-to-follow and enjoyable to read.

The information in most books is already available on the internet for free if you search hard enough for it. What makes a book valuable is that it takes all this unorganized information and lays it out in an easy to understand manner. A good book will save someone dozens or hundreds of hours scavenging through the internet and putting the pieces together themself.

Even the information in this book exists somewhere on the internet, but you won't find it explained in this manner or laid out in a step-by-step system.

Where I always like to start when creating my outline is by looking at the table of contents of other best-selling/top-rated books in my niche. You don't have to buy the book to see this because every book on Amazon has a "look inside" feature where you can see the Table of Contents and the first couple of pages of Chapter 1.

Below is an image showing where you can find this "look inside" feature to see the table of contents for any book on Amazon ... for free!

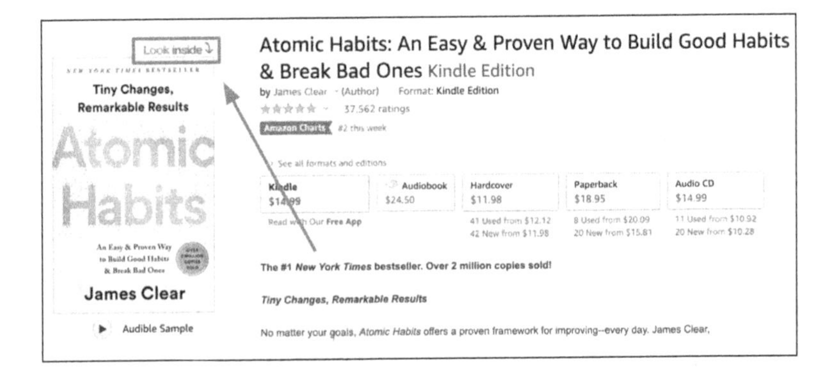

This way, you can get a very good idea of the range of content to cover in your book. There's proof of concept because we already know readers like this book.

An important topic that needs to be covered here is plagiarism. Be aware that no one owns any ideas, they just own the way that idea is expressed. As long as your writer isn't reading another book and stealing their words, the content will be very different, even if it is on the same topic. I still recommend running your writer's work through a plagiarism scanner like Grammarly, at least for the first few chapters until you build trust with your ghostwriter.

Once you have a general framework for the content you want your writer to include in your book, the next step is going out and finding the information. Using Google and YouTube as search platforms, you essentially have access to most of the information in the world. If you enjoy the topic of your book, learning all about it is actually lots of fun.

Grab a cup of coffee, put on noise-cancelling headphones, and play some relaxing study music. This really helps you to get in the zone and stay focused.

Take note of the relevant information you like. All you need to do is provide your writer with a link to the page or video and perhaps some ideas you'd like them to know. Remember to keep these links because you will need them for your citations page at the end of the book.

Citing research studies in your books is a good practice too because it provides credibility and validity to the information.

From my experience of hiring several writers over many years, I've learned that most of them like to be given a clear roadmap, but they also want creative freedom to write the book in their own way. I've had writers say no to projects because the outline had too much detail. Give them a general roadmap with complete freedom to write the book the way they want. That's their job. They're professionals, and they generally don't need your help.

Your writer will ask for a ballpark figure for how many words the book should be. The answer: As many words as you need to help the reader solve their problem. It sounds like a cop-out answer, but it's just true. Now, if you want a ballpark estimate, let's say anywhere between 15,000 and 35,000 words. It really depends on the topic, so look at the other books in your niche.

Providing a clear, well-researched outline for your writer is the best way to assure that your book will end up being something you're proud of that really makes a difference in the lives of your readers. The result will be a consistent inflow of 5-star reviews that show other readers your book is worth buying.

Arnaud is a Frenchman who joined our Audiobook Income Academy program in 2018 and now travels the world with complete freedom because of the 6-figure income he makes from his publishing business. He recently celebrated reaching 50,000 audiobooks sold and shared this tip in our private Facebook community:

Taking time to work on the outlines makes a BIG difference. This writer sent me a masterpiece I know will bring me 5- and 4-star organic reviews. Do the work. It will pay out over time!

Arnaud ...

Taking time to work on the outlines makes a BIG difference.

This writer sent me a masterpiece I know will bring me 5-4 stars organic reviews..

Do the work, it will pay out overtime! Thanks for the amazing lessons **Christian** & **Rasmus**

If, for whatever reason, you would also like to outsource the writing of your book outline, my wife started a service for publishers that does exactly that. While I believe it's a valuable learning experience to write at least your first outline yourself, I still want to present you with this option. You can check out her services at services.publishinglife.com. They have a team of 20+ writers, and they do a better job than anyone else out there.

PAYING FOR A GHOSTWRITER IS AN INVESTMENT THAT PAYS FOR ITSELF AND PROPELS YOU AND YOUR FINANCIAL SITUATION FORWARD.

19 HOW MILLIONAIRES VIEW MONEY

Cash flow is a true battle every new entrepreneur will encounter and most likely struggle with in the beginning. When first starting, it's common to perform a juggling act between paying the bills and investing in your business. And that's okay! That's completely normal, and it's to be expected. The sooner you understand that, the sooner you can stop giving in to the excuse, "I can't get started because I don't have a lot of money."

The majority of not just publishers but entrepreneurs in every industry started with very little. After all, most people choose to start a business so they can make more money because they don't have enough. Starting a business and investing in your future is something to be very proud of.

I want to share a very valuable lesson I learned about money when I first started publishing. As kids, we grew up in a small town in New Jersey, and every summer break when school was out, we had three months of absolutely nothing to do where we just had to entertain ourselves in any way possible. Since we needed (yes, needed!) money to buy video games and candy, we came up with the original idea to make a lemonade stand in the neighborhood.

This gave our dad a chance to teach us a little lesson about how running a successful business works. He said the formula for running a business is very simple: Income minus expenses equals profit.

Income is all the money we would get when people bought a cup of lemonade. So if we sold 20 cups of lemonade for $1, that's $20 of income.

Then he explained that expenses are all the costs that come with starting the lemonade stand. The cost of lemons, sugar, plastic cups, and a sign would all be expenses. These costs are bad, and we want to avoid them as much as we can.

He said the most successful lemonade stand is the one with the most income and the least expenses. So he suggested that we use the cups we already had in the house, the leftover lemonade powder in the pantry, and a piece of cardboard for the sign. That way, we could get up and running for no cost (to us) at all.

Well, we never managed to have the most successful lemonade stand. Not because we couldn't sell lots of lemonade, but we would just run out. While we were stingy with our costs, our neighborhood competitors were slinging cups left and right because they invested in ample supplies and didn't have to worry about running out.

I carried my dad's idea of "keep expenses as low as possible" around with me until my 20s. While it is logical and true on the surface that you should strive to keep expenses low, it's a crippling mindset to have when it comes time to run a real business.

My thinking was: inflow of money = good, outflow of money = bad. If I am spending money, then money is leaving me and never to return, which is bad. This led me to make some not-so-smart decisions in my first business—my electric bike drop-shipping store—like deciding not to spend money on advertising. I thought, *Why spend money to get traffic to my store when I can keep that money and just do it the free way?*

Now, I understand that not all outflow is created equally because some outflow creates inflow.

You know the quote, "you have to spend money to make money"? It's true and that's what I'm talking about.

I should have spent money on advertising, and instead of viewing it as an expense, it was actually an investment because it would have led to more money coming in than what was going out.

That's the difference between poor people and rich people. Poor people spend their money on expenses, while rich people spend their money on investments. So the next time you are about to spend your money, take a minute and think about what you will get in return. Is it an expense, or is it an investment?

A nice car, coffee, beer, restaurant food, new TV, these random things are all expenses. However, spending money on real estate, the stock market, and getting books created are all investments that make you more money.

Paying a ghostwriter is not a cost of doing business that you would want to keep as small as possible. It is an investment that pays for itself and propels you and your financial situation forward. Something may seem expensive on the surface, but it may not be once you consider what you will get in return.

What's the cost of investing to have a book written? Anywhere between $500 to $1000. What's the cost of not investing to have a book written? Well, the cost is your goals, your freedom, and many thousands of dollars in the future that you could have made if you had invested.

As Charlotte said inside of the private AIA Facebook group:

> *I never talk about how grateful I am for my publishing business. Once again, I haven't released any new books or audiobooks for the last six months, and I make consistently $5K to $6K USD per month, straight into my bank account.*
>
> *MY BIGGEST LESSON FOR YOU HERE:*
>
> *Do not f*ing be scared to invest money in yourself or your business if you know you can back yourself up and can get results. Why would you even be scared to invest $1K into a book, when you are [practically] GUARANTEED it will bring you back more than $1K? That's stupid to think it's not even worth the investment.*

Charlotte
30 January at 06:48

I never talk about how grateful I am for my publishing business.

Once again, I haven't released any new books or audiobooks for the last 6 months and I make consistently $5-6k USD a month, straight into my bank account.

MY BIGGEST LESSON FOR YOU HERE:

Do not f[ ]ing be scared to invest money in yourself or your business if you know you can back yourself up and can get results. Why would you even be scared to invest $1k into a book, when you are GUARANTEED it will bring you back MORE than $1k. That's stupid to think its not even worth the investment.

You need to spend money to make money. There are no two ways around it. If you don't have some leftover money right now, then get a job, work more hours, and spend less money on pointless sh*t that doesn't make you money.

The majority of our successful publishing students started with very little money. I'd even say you're at an advantage when you have a lack of funds because you have no other choice but to make it work. You freaking want it way more than someone who already has some money.

If you continue to do what you've always done, you'll continue to get what you've always got. Change how you view investments in a business because they are what ignites and propels every successful business forward.

20 THE GHOSTWRITING PROCESS

Your outline is done and ready to be handed off to a writer. At this stage, you have two options for finding a ghost-writer:

1) Ghostwriting company

2) Freelance writer

A ghostwriting company is exactly as it seems—a company with its own team of vetted and trained writers (sometimes 100+ of them) that offers ghostwriting as a service.

Pros of using a ghostwriting company:

- Easy to use: This is definitely the biggest benefit of using a ghostwriting company. It's just so easy and low stress. You go on their website, pick a package, give them your book title and outline, and they'll assign the writer they believe is best fit for the job.

- Great customer support: The ghostwriting company will work as a mediator between you and your writer, so if there is anything with the book you are unsatisfied with, they will almost always go the distance to make you happy.

Cons of using a ghostwriting company:

- Quality can vary: There can be a wide range of talent among writers ranging from very skilled to below average to inadequate. With ghostwriting companies, it is especially important to get the first chapter back from your writer before continuing the writing of the book.
- Working with a middleman: Since there is a middleman involved between you and the writer, it means they need to take a cut and therefore charge a slightly higher price.
- Less control over the book: Some people may see this as a benefit because it means less work, but it usually creates a higher likelihood of you being unsatisfied with the writing and revisions being needed.

Your other option is hiring a freelance writer who you work with one-on-one. There are various platforms and websites where you can search for freelance writers looking for work, but the only platform we ever use is Upwork.com. It's the biggest freelance platform in the world (more than 1,000 writers looking for work at any given time), and I've found that's where the majority of the best writers are. There's no need to go searching on any other sites. Upwork is the best.

Pros:

- The most talented writers are freelancers: The best writers prefer to work for themselves.

- Can be cheaper: Because no middleman needs to be paid, you can get great books written for a lower price.

Cons:

- Requires a hiring process: This is the biggest disadvantage to using a freelancer, but it only needs to be done once per writer. Once you find a great one, working with them becomes easy.
- Requires more responsibility from you. Because there is no ghostwriting company as a mediator, you and the writer have to agree on things like price, deadlines, and revisions.

A ghostwriting company is the easy, beginner-friendly option, but oftentimes the talent level among writers isn't quite as high.

Using a freelance writer is not as beginner-friendly because you have to hire someone, but there is a much greater likelihood of finding a great writer.

There is no right or wrong choice. In the end, you need to use your judgment to assess which is a better option for you. You can easily build a $100K/year publishing business with either one.

If you would like a list of our recommended ghostwriting companies, go to publishinglife.com/writing.

HAVING A PROFESSIONALLY DESIGNED BOOK COVER IS SOMETHING THAT WILL MAKE YOUR BOOK LOOK LIKE AN AUTHORITY PIECE.

21 HOW TO LOOK LIKE A BESTSELLER

Creating the book cover is my favorite step in the publishing process because it turns an idea in your head into something that's finally real. It's a really cool feeling when you get a copy shipped to your house for the first time and you get to hold the book in your hands and feel the smooth cover and the spine and the weight of the pages. I love it.

Having a professionally designed book cover is something that will make your book look like an authority piece. When you have an amateur book cover, it makes the entire book feel low quality and mediocre, no matter how great the inside of the book is.

High quality cover design can be pricey if you don't know any better, but I'm about to show you how to get a professional cover for your book at a price anyone can afford.

Take a look at the following six book covers. How much do you think it costs to get each of these designed?

SPEAKING 4 PROFIT
ACADEMY
SPEAKING
4 PROFIT
101
A Beginner's Guide to Public Speaking
EVOLVE BENTON

INTERMEDIATE LEVEL (A2/B1)
French
FLUENCY
JOURNEY
Audio Included
ANNA BOURGOGNE
@YOUR.DAILY.FRENCH

PREPPER'S
SURVIVAL
GUIDE
A Prepper's Quickstart Guide To
Survival and Self Sufficient Living
ALEX WILD

WEALTHY
HEALTHY
HAPPY
A PRACTICAL GUIDE HOW TO LIVE
THE LIFE YOU DESERVE
Alex Frost
ALEC MCGALLIARD
CARE
to LEAD
HOW TO MASTER AND IMPLEMENT
FOUR KEYS TO LEADERSHIP:
COMMUNICATION, ACCOUNTABILITY,
RELATIONSHIPS AND
EXAMPLE OF EXCELLENCE
THE 4 PHASE APPROACH TO
KINDLE BOOK MARKETING
SUCCESS IN 2018
BOOK
LAUNCH
GLADIATOR
JORDAN RING

$20!

The planet is overflowing with so many talented graphic designers that will work at a discount— you just need to know where to find them.

Our go-to website for finding low-cost expert cover designers is Fiverr.com. It's so cheap there because you literally have more than 1,000 cover designers offering their services, which drives the price way down. You also have many talented designers from countries like Bangladesh and the Philippines, where $20 is the equivalent of $200 for them.

When choosing which cover designer to go with, I suggest looking at each designer's portfolio of past covers they have designed. This will give you an idea of the style of covers they can create and whether you think it's a good fit for your book or not.

When you make your order, all they need is your book title, author name, and anything you would like on the cover. For example, a certain image, colors, or style. It's a great idea to send them examples of other book covers that you really like, that way, they know what you want. If you don't have any preferences, you can just give them complete creative freedom to design the cover.

When you've made your order, just relax until they deliver the first draft. Once you get it, put it side by side with other best-selling books in your niche and see how it stacks up. Your book cover can have a big influence on sales because it's really the advertisement for your book. Have a boring, home-made-looking cover, and people won't notice your book. What you want is something that stands out and portrays authority and expertise.

In Christian's case, he learned you can have a pretty bad book cover and still make consistent sales. The first book he ever published was about how to be a 4.0 GPA student, and while it's not a bestseller, it's made him a few thousand dollars in its lifetime and still sells copies every month. Here is the not-so-impressive cover again.

For a list of our recommended book cover designers, go to publishinglife.com/covers.

22 THE SECRET TO SUCCESS

"What's the key to success with publishing?"

We get asked this question a ton. Anyone that asks this question is looking for one secret thing that all the successful publishers are doing that no one else knows about. They're hoping to be told about the secret fail-proof niche or the book launch strategy all the successful ones are using. But it doesn't work like that.

To answer the question, I want to share a real-life rags to riches publishing success story with you.

Soorej is a 23-year-old guy from Bangalore, India. Life over there is nothing like it is in first-world countries like the US, UK, and Canada. The idea of creating any form of income online isn't just insane, it's nonexistent. Even for the most hardworking individuals, there is very little opportunity to create wealth as the average full-time salary is just $300 per month.

It was 2016, and Soorej had reached the age where he needed to figure out what he would do for a career and how he would make a living for himself. He knew accountants were paid an above-average salary, but he hated the idea of working 12-hour days moving numbers around in a spreadsheet. And yet, he saw no better options in India, so accounting is what he pursued.

His university studies required that he work as an intern at an accounting firm, but dozens of students were fighting to land a limited number of internships. Eight interviews and eight rejections later, he was still without a job. He studied 8 to 12 hours every day to pass his accounting exams. Two attempts and two failed exams later, he felt completely hopeless.

He had run out of all options and saw no other possible path in life, so he tried again. While studying for a third attempt to pass his accounting exam, he had lost every bit of motivation and purpose. So he went on YouTube in search of some motivational videos to lift him up. One thing led to another, and he found himself watching a video talking about how to make money by publishing books on Amazon.

After learning a bit about the process, he thought about whether this was even possible for him. With literally $0 to invest (he didn't even have a bank account), his only option was to write the books himself. Even if he wanted to write them himself, it would have to be early in the morning or late at night when he wasn't in classes or studying. To top it off, his written English was poor, given that it was his second language.

Every single factor in his life was working against him. He was completely out of options, and although success was extremely unlikely, he still saw it as a no-risk opportunity. The real risk would be doing nothing and continuing to go deeper and deeper down a path that he knew would make him miserable forever. Desperate to improve his life, and without a single thing in the world to lose, he decided to give it a try.

Soorej spent the next three months writing his first book on the topic of time management. He found someone offering book cover design on Fiverr for just $5. The problem was that he had literally zero money. So he approached his dad, who agreed to lend him $5 for cover design (Soorej has since paid him back).

Having poured blood, sweat, and tears into this book, he finally hit "publish" on Amazon. He had an initial boost in sales in the first week from friends and family, but after that, it barely sold.

He had put so much time and effort into this book, and having it produce almost nothing was extremely disappointing. But instead of thinking, *Publishing is a scam, it doesn't work,* he looked at himself in the mirror and thought, *What could I have done better?*

He took a look at his book from an objective point of view. *Well, the cover looks unprofessional, and the content inside is awful. I'm only selling the book as an ebook, and I have no reviews.*

Most other people in his position would have looked for reasons why it's not their own fault. They would blame the business model, call it quits, and move on with their lives. But Soorej was a part of a Facebook community of publishers, and he saw others having success on a daily basis. He knew it worked, he was just doing it wrong, and he blamed no one besides himself for that.

In the meantime, he was still pursuing an accounting internship because he wanted money to invest in a real writer for his books. He finally managed to land an internship, but he was utterly miserable working 12 hour days in exchange for a whopping $150 per month salary. That's $5 per day or about $0.50 per hour. He even says some days, he would show up at the office at 8 a.m. and not leave until 2 a.m. because he had certain responsibilities and could not leave until all the accounts were right.

Now, with a full-time job combined with studying for exams, any time to write his book was virtually gone. He had reached a stage of depression and a new low point in his life.

He spent the next year writing books himself while he saved up money to invest in a writer. Any spare moment he had, he would spend it writing, or else it was never going to get done.

Seven months later, he launched his second book. Unfortunately, the result was the same as the first. But he knew with certainty he was doing something wrong or else the book would be selling.

After more failed writing attempts, he had wasted over a year writing books himself with no guidance. While anyone else would have viewed that year as a waste of time, Soorej says the knowledge and publishing experience he gained was invaluable.

He had finally saved up enough money to pay for a writer, and he took everything he had learned from his past failures and applied it to this book.

He launched it once again, and after the initial sales boost from his friends and family, it continued to sell. Some positive reviews had come in, and then more people started buying the book. Soorej was in disbelief and awe, but didn't waste any time and released more books on the same topic.

Eleven months and six books later, Soorej hit his first $10,000 month in November 2018.

So what is the key to success with publishing?

Commitment and determination.

Commitment to the process, commitment to yourself and the determination to overcome obstacles that come in your way. Anyone who is not committed and gives up at the first sign of resistance will not have success with a publishing business. Well, any business for that matter. Well, ANYTHING for that matter.

Soorej did not have an easy journey. He was not a one-hit-wonder. He didn't get lucky the first time. He had all the odds stacked against him, but he was so determined and committed to improving his life that he was not going to let any of his disadvantages stop him.

When Soorej figured it out, he went from $0 to $10,000 per month and the top 0.001% in India in one year. He went from hopeless and depressed to buying his dream motorcycle, a Kawasaki Ninja, for $15,000. He even had to call up one of his friends and ask, "What do I do with all this money?!"

Whenever you are feeling hopeless or unmotivated, think of Soorej. If he can do it working and studying full time in India making $150 a month with English as his second language, you can do it too.

A quick funny story ... When Christian and I met up with Soorej in Bali in 2018, the first thing he said to us was, "You are the first white people I've ever met in my entire life." What an honor. Thank you, Soorej!

I know Soorej's story sounds unbelievable, so if you want to hear it all told from his mouth, we did a video interview with him in Bali in 2018 just after he had hit his first $10,000 month. You can watch the interview at publishinglife.com/soorej.

I'm very excited to say that exactly two years after this interview, Soorej had his first $100,000 month in his business. He now has a team of writers, a designer, a manager, and more. Congratulations, Soorej. You deserve every bit of success that you have.

End-of-Module Roundup

In this module, you learned that anyone can create books and audiobooks by outsourcing all the hard stuff to skilled experts.

You learned that ghostwriting is one of the most common practices in the book publishing world. It is done often by celebrities, regular successful publishers like you and me, and even James Patterson.

You learned about low-cost expert outsourcing. You can affordably outsource the elements that take the most time and expertise, which are:

1) the writing,

2) the book cover, and

3) the narration of your book.

You learned that a good book title is about ranking and persuasion. Your title must include keywords and speak about the goal people want to achieve when they buy your book.

You learned that reviews play a big role in the long-term success of your book. Your reviews are dependent on the quality of the book. A good book will set a positive feedback loop in motion and lead to consistent long-term sales.

You learned that a great book comes from a well-researched book outline. Creating a well-researched book outline is only a matter of sitting down and doing the work. You'll have fun with this part if the niche you choose is something you enjoy.

You learned that poor people spend their money on expenses, while rich people spend their money on investments so they can make more money. Publishing costs are investments.

You learned that the cost of investing to have a book written ($500-$800) is far less than the cost of not investing to have a book written (your goals, your freedom, and many thousands of dollars in the future). Something that may seem expensive on the surface is actually cheap when you consider what you get in return.

You learned that the two options you have for ghostwriting are a ghostwriting company or a freelance writer. And you learned the pros and cons of each. Using a ghostwriting company is easier, but you can get a lower rate and oftentimes a better book when you use a freelance writer.

You learned that your book cover plays a big role in how readers will judge your book. If your book cover is good, the inside of your book will also be perceived as good and vice versa.

You learned how to get a professionally designed book cover for only $20.

Most importantly, you learned that the true secret to success with publishing is simple. It's a matter of committing and not giving up, even when it feels hard. The good things in life do not come without adversity.

You learned that if Soorej can do it, so can you.

In the next module, we will show you how to launch your books the right way so that Amazon and Audible will push your book to their millions of readers and listeners for you.

MODULE 4

LAUNCH

23 THE BIGGEST CHEAT CODE IN ONLINE BUSINESS

Now, we're onto the launch phase of your book.

A product launch is often the most challenging (and stressful) part of any business because it involves the one thing almost no one likes to do: Selling.

It's no wonder because it ain't easy. Any other online business will require you to either hop on the phone and convince the person to buy your product or service, or you have to run ads and learn sales psychology to convince them why they should buy your thing.

Yet another reason why I chose to get into Amazon book publishing in the first place is you don't have to deal with any of that. When you decide to sell on Amazon's platform, you're essentially agreeing to a partnership with Amazon where you bring the content (books and audiobooks) and they sell it for you. You're working side by side with them to achieve the same goal ... Sell as many damn books as possible!

And who knows better how to sell stuff online than Amazon? No one.

The biggest cheat code in online business is being able to (no, *they want you to*) tap into Amazon's base of over 200 million customers. While others have to spend years learning SEO or hoping to break even using Facebook ads, we're just over here making easy sales to Amazon's customers.

Plus, EVERYONE trusts Amazon, which is more important than ever when most people's first thought before buying anything online is *Is this a scam? Can I trust this seller?* Not with Amazon. In fact, 89% of buyers agree that they're more likely to buy products from Amazon than other e-commerce sites.[6]

Fun fact: Did you know 82% of US households have an Amazon Prime account?[7]

"Amazon does the selling for you" sounds great and all, but what does that really mean? As I explained in an earlier chapter, Amazon will show your book to potential customers that search for books about your topic on Amazon and Audible. They'll browse through the search results and often buy multiple books about that topic. This buying process happens on its own, continuously, 24/7/365 at a massive scale on Amazon *and* Audible without you needing to lift a finger.

This is how Christian made over $50,000 in six months without even logging in to his Amazon account. That's just what it's like selling books and audiobooks on Amazon. Another student of ours, Alessandro, decided he didn't want to work for seven months, and he still made over $5,500 in a month:

---

6 Maryam Mohsin, "10 Amazon Statistics You Need to Know in 2021 [March 2021]," Oberlo (Oberlo, May 16, 2021), https://www.oberlo.com/blog/amazon-statistics.

7 CNN, "Smerconish: Amazon Was Primed for a Pandemic," YouTube (YouTube, November 28, 2020), https://www.youtube.com/watch?t=129&v=mIeMe9tZof8&feature=youtu.be.

And it's because Amazon sells for you.

Now, you can't just upload your book to Amazon and Audible, do nothing, sit back and expect money to flow in. There's a launch process to it and steps you need to take before this automated buying process can set in, but once you have gone through the launch process Amazon takes over and does the selling for you. That is when this business becomes truly passive for years and years to come.

This launch process is what I'll be showing you in this module. Let's do this.

BOOK REVIEWS ARE SOCIAL PROOF WHICH IS ONE OF THE MOST PERSUASIVE BUYING FACTORS.

24 THE LAUNCH BLUEPRINT

People have a way of making almost everything in life a lot more complicated than it needs to be. We think because someone achieved amazing results, there must be a complex and intricate strategy to it that no one else knows about. That's often not the case.

We've tried almost every strategy there is when it comes to launching your book. While some of the strategies were a complete waste of time, some of them worked pretty well. I could make this launch process very complex by telling you to set up campaigns with a dozen book promotion websites, reach out to influencers to do an email list cross-promotion, and then set up some Facebook retargeting ads. While those strategies can definitely be helpful, the difference they make is only marginal compared to what I'm about to show you.

Whether you're launching a book on Amazon or an audiobook on Audible, there is one thing you should put all of your focus on because it will give you a bigger ROI (return on investment) than anything else. Without this one thing, you will struggle to sell books. But *with* this one thing, sales will truly be automatic. That thing is ... reviews.

The effect that reviews have on book sales is twofold.

1) Lots of positive reviews on a book is a signal to Amazon that this is a great book that many people are buying and enjoying. Then Amazon and Audible will push that book up the search rankings and show it to more and more people. That's just how the Amazon and Audible algorithms work. They will promote the books that people like, and reviews are what tells them that.

2) The other major impact reviews have on book sales is with regards to buyer psychology.Think about the last time you bought something online. Did you buy it blindly, or did you check the reviews first to see if past buyers were happy with their purchase?

Book reviews are social proof which is one of the most persuasive buying factors. It reassures shoppers that your book is worth buying. If a book has no reviews, the shopper feels like they are taking a risk because there's no proof others liked the book. If a book has a majority of negative reviews, that's a clear sign this book is not worth buying, and then Amazon will push it down the rankings.

Here are two identical books shown side-by-side. Everything is exactly the same about these two books, except the reviews. The first book has 7 reviews and a 4-star average rating and the second book has 363 reviews and a 5-star average rating. Which one are you more likely to pick up and read?

The second book is much more appealing than the other, isn't it? Even though it's the exact same book.

These two factors combined are why reviews are our #1 focus during the launch phase. If I were to simplify what a super-profitable book looks like, it's this:

Solid niche + good title with keywords + good cover +
100 or more positive book reviews
= passive income machine for many years to come.

As I explained in a previous chapter, the quality of your book's content is critical, but I didn't include that in the equation because it goes hand in hand with book reviews. You can only have 100+ positive reviews if your book is of high quality.

After the launch phase when you have a good chunk of positive reviews, the book will start to sell consistently on its own. From there on, just let Amazon and Audible work their magic. You won't have to do anything because the positive reviews will just come in on their own. If you're a part of the 99 percent who has bought something on Amazon before, you'll notice they send out reminder emails a few days after buying a product asking you to leave a review.

Now the reason why some people struggle to sell books is because they find themselves stuck in a catch-22 situation. You can't sell many books without getting reviews, but you can't get reviews without selling many books.

If you don't know any better, that's true. But having been in this game for many years now, we have nailed the art of getting reviews during a book launch, even before any book sales come in. And it's something anyone can do regardless of experience, knowledge, skills, connections, or anything else. Let's talk all about it in the next chapter.

Speaking of how important reviews are...

You may be feeling an uncontrollable urge right now to go on Amazon, find *The Freedom Shortcut*, and leave a glowing honest review.

If that's how you feel, I won't stop you. I'll even save you the 20 seconds it takes to search for the book on Amazon. Just click this link instead:

https://www.amazon.com/gp/product/B097CJK4W9

If you're reading this book on paper or listening to the audiobook, then I can't help you. You'll just have to find the book yourself. Sorry!

Whether you're feeling the urge or not, here's a friendly nudge to leave a review for this book if 1) you've taken some form of value from it or 2) you're just a nice person that likes to support others.

Onto the next chapter where I show you how to get reviews! Other than asking for it midbook like I just did (definitely do that too because it works).

YOU CAN BE
FINANCIALLY SET
FOR THE REST OF
YOUR LIFE WITH
JUST 1 BOOK IF
IT HAS 1,000+
REVIEWS. THAT'S
A BOOK THAT WILL
NEVER EVER STOP
SELLING.

25

THE EASY 100+ REVIEW METHOD

You can use many different methods to get book reviews on Amazon and Audible, but the big problem is that they're almost all capped. If you want to use your network, it may work to get five to ten reviews, but once you run out of people, now what? You're stuck.

What I love about the outreach review method is that it's simple, it's repeatable, it's completely free, it works for anyone in any niche, and best of all, it's scalable. Meaning, if you can use this method to get five reviews, you can get 100 reviews. You would just need to repeat the same steps 20 times.

All it takes to do this is a little grunt work. It's easy, and it works, but it's a little boring. Many people spend most of their day working a job that they dislike or is boring, so I'm sure you can dedicate a few hours to this given what the reward is.

It's like if I put 1,000 bottles of water in front of you and told you to open them all. It would be tedious and time-consuming, and you probably wouldn't want to do it, but you easily *could*. Anyone could. If I told you opening those 1,000 water bottles would create a consistent stream of monthly income for you, I'm sure you would have no problem doing it.

Well, that's what this is.

The basis of the outreach review method is very simple. You're simply reaching out to people online that fit your target audience and then offering your book to them for free. This doesn't cost you anything because you will simply send them an ebook version of your book and not a print copy.

I want to specify that it is technically against Amazon's Terms of Service to require a review in exchange for a free book copy. Meaning you can't say, "I'll give you a free copy if you leave a review." To stay compliant, you must give your book for free and then present them the option to leave a review if they feel your book is deserving of one. As long as your book is helpful to them, they will be more than happy to leave you a glowing 5-star review.

So where do you find people to give your book to for free? The answer is wherever your target audience hangs out online.

If you go on Facebook and search for groups in your niche, you will most likely find many groups with thousands or tens of thousands of people in them all interested in the topic of your book. If you go on Instagram, there are certain accounts that your target audience is following by the thousands. There's LinkedIn, Twitter, and other platforms too. Over the next 100 years, the most popular platforms will continue to change, and that's completely fine. Each platform may work a little differently than the next, but in the end, it's all the same. It's just a matter of getting in contact with your target audience.

You have the ability to reach out to all these people and start a dialogue. You don't want to come in hot and spam people with messages like, "Will you review my book?! Can you please leave a review?!" People hate that and will ignore you every time. But if you start a genuine conversation with them and once you've built a rapport, casually mention that you're launching a book, and many people will be ecstatic to get your book for free. They're often honored when the author (even though you didn't write the book, YOU are the author) of a published book reaches out to them, asking to read it before it's released. They think it's super cool.

Gathering reviews for your book is a bit tedious, but it's a simple rinse and repeat process. It's the exact method our students that are making passive full-time income are using. Do you want to make consistent income from your books so you can eventually quit your job? Then start reaching out!

Do you need 100+ reviews on a book for it to sell a lot of copies? Not at all. You can absolutely have a book that brings in over $1,000 per month consistently with fewer than 50 reviews, *but* I want your books to make as much money every month as humanly possible.

And we've found that once you break that 100 review threshold, you're close to guaranteeing yourself a passive income machine that keeps producing month after month and year after year. Less than 100 reviews and you're losing out on sales and not maximizing your income from each book. We don't want that.

It is absolutely a case of "the more reviews, the better." The more reviews your books have, the more money they will make for you. I mean this **literally.** Even once you cross 100 reviews and you move on to the next book, don't stop focusing on reviews. It is one of the easiest ways to increase your income from each book.

The more reviews you have, the more your books will sell, and the more organic reviews your books will get. Organic reviews are ones that just happen on their own without you doing anything. It's that awesome positive feedback loop.

Over time, you can have a book with over 1,000 reviews. Yes, that's a big number. Yes, it will take at least 1-2 years to get there. Yes, it will require consistent effort.

But I am not being hyperbolic when I say that you can be financially set for the rest of your life with just one book if it has 1,000+ reviews. That's a book that will never ever stop selling.

AUDIO CREATION

When we quit our jobs and started traveling the world, we had never created an audiobook, nor had we done any of the methods I'll be showing you in Module 5 to multiply your publishing income. It was literally just the bare essentials we were doing. I say that to tell you that everything I've covered up until now is plenty to go out and make full-time income selling books on Amazon.

The fun part is that we're just scratching the surface with what you can do in your publishing business, and it starts with audiobooks.

Even today, there are more than 100 times as many books on Amazon as there are audiobooks on Audible. For some reason, people aren't turning their books into audiobooks, and I believe it's because most think it's expensive and time consuming, so they don't even try. But hey, I won't complain because it leaves people like you and me with a wide-open, blue-ocean opportunity to dominate on Audible.

The truth is that once your book is created, the hardest part is over. You have this awesome piece of content created, and if you're not turning your book into an audiobook, you're leaving so much money on the table it's not even funny.

A book is something you only have to create once, then you can sell it and make money with it forever. With the audiobook, you're adding a completely separate, brand spanking new stream of income to EVERY book you publish. All you have to do is convert it to audio!

Audiobooks are the hottest selling format right now, but you'll notice there aren't many chapters in this book talking specifically about audiobooks. Even though they'll make up a huge chunk of your publishing earnings, there's just not that much to say because publishing audiobooks is so quick and easy.

To get started, you need to sign up for an account with ACX (Audiobook Creation Exchange), the official audiobook publishing platform for Audible.

Bravo to Amazon for creating such an easy-to-use and streamlined platform for getting books narrated into audio. They have a massive base of over 300,000 narrators (according to ACX.com) to choose from and make it super simple for you to filter narrators by gender, language, price, accent, vocal style, vocal age, and more.

To avoid the overwhelm of sifting through 300,000 different narrators, I suggest filtering by gender, language, and price, and if there are still too many options to choose from, filter by accent as well. That should get you down to a few hundred or a few thousand narrators to choose from. Then just start lis-

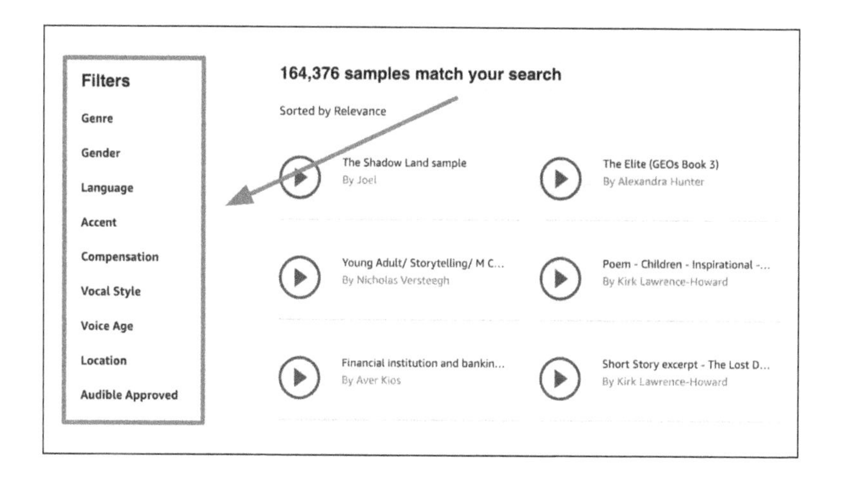

tening to each narrator's samples to hear what their voice and tone are like.

When you find a narrator you like, just send them a message asking if they'd like to narrate your audiobook. If they agree, you just send them the manuscript to your book, and your work is done. Within 1-2 weeks, they will deliver your audiobook's completed narration in high-end studio quality.

No matter your price range, ACX has the perfect narrator for you. Pricing is listed on a PFH (per finished hour) basis, which means you only pay for every minute of recorded audio narration. If your narrator charges $50 PFH and your audiobook is 3 hours long, your cost is $150. This is a really standard price for audio narration; in fact, when we first started getting our books narrated, we were paying $30-$40 PFH. We would usually make back that cost in the first month of our audiobook being live on Audible.

If you're so strapped for cash that you can't drop $100 to create a new stream of passive income, that's okay. However, it's not a valid reason not to take action because there is actually a little trick you can use where you don't have to pay a single penny for narration.

When you're listing your audiobook for narration on ACX, you can choose to pay the narrator upfront for their work, OR you can pay them nothing upfront and instead share 50% of all royalties earned by that audiobook with the narrator.

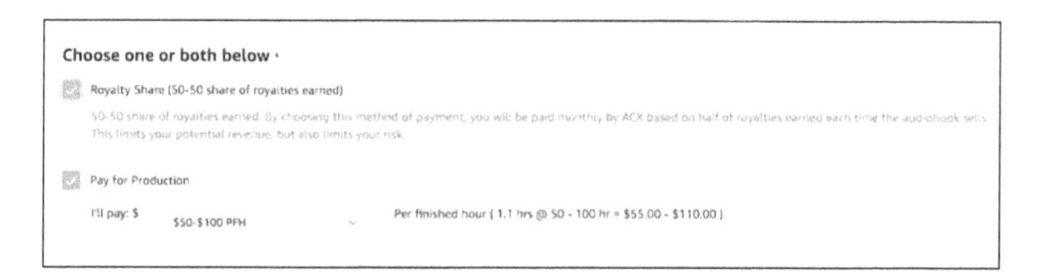

So the question is, should you pay upfront or choose the royalty share option? Let me tell you a little story.

One of our best friends in the world, Ollie (who wrote the foreword to this book), started publishing in 2017, and it completely changed his life the same way it did for us. His publishing business has given him complete freedom in life and allowed him to live all over the world in Bali, Mexico, Korea, and more.

When he had his first audiobooks narrated, he was struggling for cash like most others. He was skeptical his audiobook would even sell at all, so when he saw the opportunity to pay nothing for narration, he hopped on it. *I've got nothing to lose,* is what he thought.

When the audiobook went live on Audible, it started selling instantly, and Ollie was thrilled. He realized his publishing business's huge potential once he would get all his books narrated into audiobooks. But as the audiobook started selling more and more, it became more and more painful because he knew only half of each sale belonged to him. The other half was going to the narrator.

I wanted to be sure I got the numbers right, so I sent a message to Ollie as I was writing this chapter asking him how much he has lost because he chose to do a royalty share for that one audiobook.

He replied within a few minutes. Here was his response.

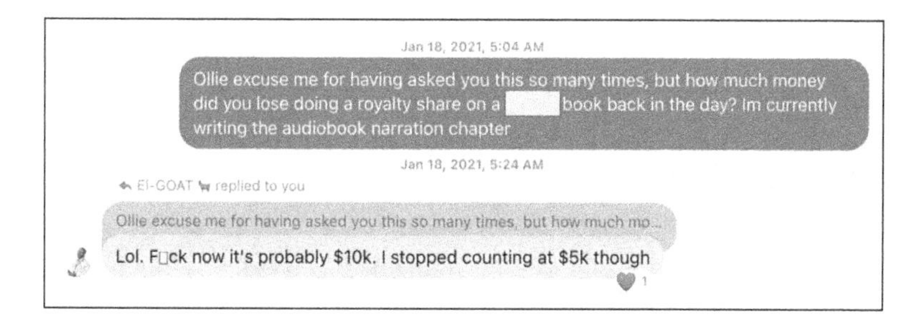

Instead of paying $150 upfront for narration, Ollie has paid about $10,000 to that narrator. And he will continue to pay him next month and the month after and so on. Each royalty share agreement with a narrator lasts for seven years, so the torture won't end for a few more years.

You can see why royalty shares are the most sought after deals for narrators. Anyone, even the best narrators on ACX, are dying to find a chump willing to do a royalty share with them. Narrators know how much these audiobooks sell, and they want a piece.

So my advice to you, even if you don't have $150 to spend, NEVER take a royalty share with a narrator. Instead, just wait, save up, and pay them upfront when you have the money. It's better to wait a few months than to share 50 percent of your roy-

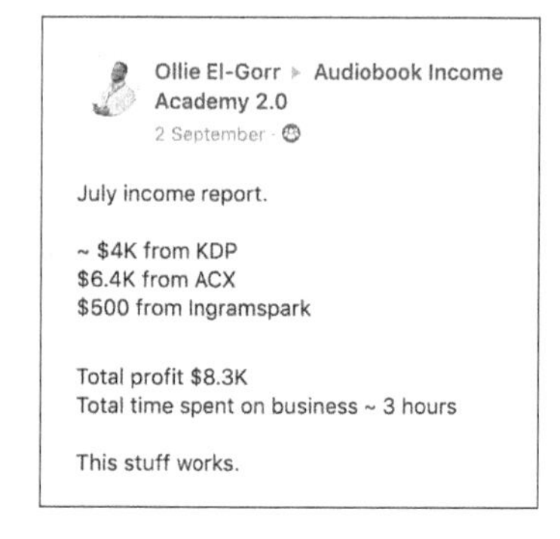

alties with the narrator because you will always end up losing money, likely thousands of dollars over the years.

As I said, it hasn't been all bad for Ollie. Here's a screenshot of his July 2019 income report: approximately $4K from KDP, $6.4 from ACX, and $500 from IngramSpark. His total profit was $8.3K for approximately three hours of work.

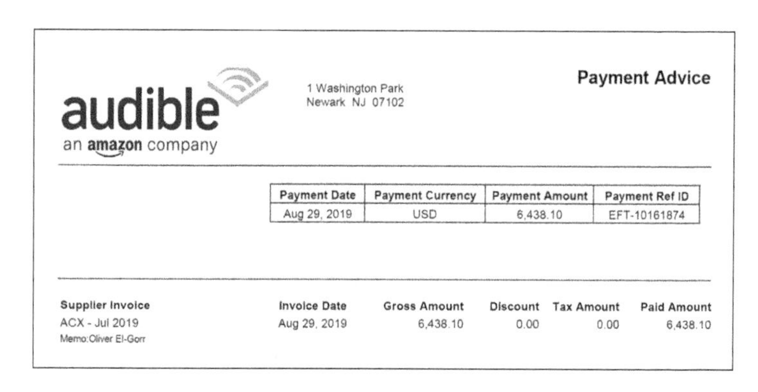

audible
an amazon company

1 Washington Park
Newark NJ 07102

Payment Advice

Payment Date	Payment Currency	Payment Amount	Payment Ref ID
Aug 29, 2019	USD	6,438.10	EFT-10161874

Supplier Invoice	Invoice Date	Gross Amount	Discount	Tax Amount	Paid Amount
ACX - Jul 2019 Memo:Oliver El-Gorr	Aug 29, 2019	6,438.10	0.00	0.00	6,438.10

Not bad, indeed.

AUDIO LAUNCH

This is going to be a very short chapter. The reason why is because you're using the exact same strategy when launching your audiobook as when you're launching your book on Amazon. The same principles apply.

It's all about reviews, and once you have that initial bunch of reviews from the launch phase, Audible takes over and does all the selling for you, in true passive fashion. There are just a few minor differences you should know, which I'll get into now.

Something ACX offers is free promo codes for every audiobook you publish—100 of them, to be exact. These are codes that ANYONE can enter into Audible to get your audiobook free instead of paying the full price. ACX gives these codes to you for the sole purpose of making the process of collecting reviews much easier.

The first people you want to reach out to for audiobook reviews are the people that already left reviews for your book on Amazon. They already love your book, so just send them a free code, and most will be very happy to leave another review.

Another easy way to distribute these codes for reviews is by going into a Facebook group and offering the admin to share 50–100 free copies of your audiobook with their group members. If you ask in the right way by framing it as you doing something that benefits their group members (which you are, but it's also for your own benefit, just don't say that), then most will happily say yes.

And there you go. You just added a second HUGE stream of income to each book you publish, and all you spent was a tiny bit of money and effort to do so. That's smart business.

End-of-Module Roundup

You learned how much easier it is to run a business with Amazon on your side doing most of the work and selling for you.

You learned how publishing is truly passive income—unlike almost all other online businesses. It's because the process of people finding your book and buying it on Amazon and Audible is fully automated and happens all on its own.

You learned how easy it is to find a narrator for your audiobook using ACX.

You learned that audio narration for a whole book can cost $150 or less. It can even be free if you choose to do a royalty share, but you will always lose money in the long run by doing that.

You learned how to launch your audiobook on Audible. It's very similar to your book launch on Amazon, except ACX gives you promo codes, which makes getting reviews for your audiobook even easier.

You learned what the most important thing is to focus on during your book launch. **Reviews.**

You learned exactly how to get as many reviews as you want for no cost at all. It's not hard, but it's tedious and a matter of repeating the same process over and over.

Now onto Module 5 where I'll share how you can multiply your income from each book.

MODULE 5

MULTIPLY

28 THE FUN STUFF

So far, we've only covered the fundamentals of Amazon book publishing. The fundamentals are never exciting, but they are the bare minimum needed to make full-time income with this business.

Yet, we are still just scratching the surface. Now we can dive into the fun stuff and the ninja tactics we use to multiply our publishing income and squeeze every last dollar out of each book we publish.

If I were to use an analogy, Modules 1 through 4 show you how to start a fire, which is the hardest part. Module 5 is where I show you how to pour gasoline all over that fire and multiply the money you make from your books and audiobooks.

I kid you not—if you take action on everything I'm about to share, I don't see how you're not making full-time income from your books within 12 months. But that's the key, of course. You need to actually implement and do what I'm about to tell you *because it is life-changing*. If you don't actually apply this stuff, it is utterly useless.

Let's get to it.

BUNDLING IS ONE OF THE MOST COMMON AND EFFECTIVE STRATEGIES AUTHORS USE TO MAKE MORE MONEY WITHOUT CREATING MORE BOOKS.

29 A GIFT FROM THE MONEY GODS

This method of multiplying your income from each book is something James Patterson, J.K. Rowling, and all the other best sellers in the world have been doing since the very beginning, and they are all masters of it.

It's a strategy they use to publish more books without writing more books. How is that even possible?

What I'm talking about is what we like to call bundles. Also known as a box set, collection, series, or compilation of books.

No matter what you call it, it all means the same thing. It's two or more books combined and sold as one completely separate new book. You can make a two-book bundle, three-book bundle, five-book bundle, ten-book bundle, etc.

In the interview with Patrick Jackson at publishinglife.com/patrick, he was asked which strategies he learned from us had the biggest impact on his publishing business. He answered, "Bundles. They had a huge impact on my business. It just changed everything."

We always jokingly call bundles the "gift from the money gods" because that's exactly what it feels like. It's a fast, easy, and nearly free way to get more money out of every book you publish.

Let's have a look at one of James Patterson's book bundles.

This bundle is a brand new book he sells, and all he did was take five of his already existing books and combine them into one. On top of that, he's able to charge more and make more on each sale of his bundles.

Something we and our students have found is that bundles often sell even more copies than the single books included within that bundle. This is especially the case with audiobooks. Here's why: The price of an audiobook on Audible is based solely on the length of the audiobook. Here you can see the pricing model they use:

Length	Price
under 1 hour	$3.95
1 - 3 hours	$6.95
3 - 5 hours	$14.95
5 - 10 hours	$19.95
10 - 20 hours	$24.95
over 20 hour	$29.95

A 3-hour long audiobook is priced at $14.95. If you create a bundle of two 3-hour long audiobooks, then you have one 6-hour long audiobook bundle priced at $19.95. You're getting $29.90 ($14.95 x 2) worth of value for just $19.95, a nice 33% discount for customers. That's why bundles are a better deal and more enticing to customers, causing them to often sell more than singles.

In the interview with Patrick Jackson, he was asked if his bundles sell more than his singles. And his exact words were, "Yes, definitely."

Another perk is that creating bundles lowers your financial investment per book.

Let's say it costs $600 to get one book ghostwritten. If you have two books written for $600 each and you're smart enough to bundle them, you then have a third book you can publish at no additional cost as an ebook, print book and audiobook. In reality, the investment for ghostwriting isn't $600 per book; it's actually only $400 per book because you're getting three for the price of two.

And it goes fast! There's no waiting for a third book to be done because all the content is already written.

Bundling is one of the most common and effective strategies authors use to make more money without creating more books. James Patterson and J.K. Rowling do this for all their books.

You lower your costs and increase your earnings per book while giving customers more buying options.

30

MAXIMIZING INCOME STREAMS

One of the beautiful things about books is that once a book is written and created, you now have an asset that can create many income streams with minimal added effort. The bulk of the effort comes from writing the book itself, which you hire a professional to do for you.

For your books to reach as many customers as possible, they need to be available for sale on as many online bookstores as possible.

While Amazon and Audible are by far the biggest and most popular online bookstores in the world, they are far from the only ones. There is a percentage of the market that only shops on lesser-known online book stores.

If you're only publishing your books on Amazon and Audible, you're only reaching 60% of the market. The other 40% is comprised of many online bookstores like Barnes & Noble, Apple Books, Google Play Books, Powell's Books, Kobo, and many more.

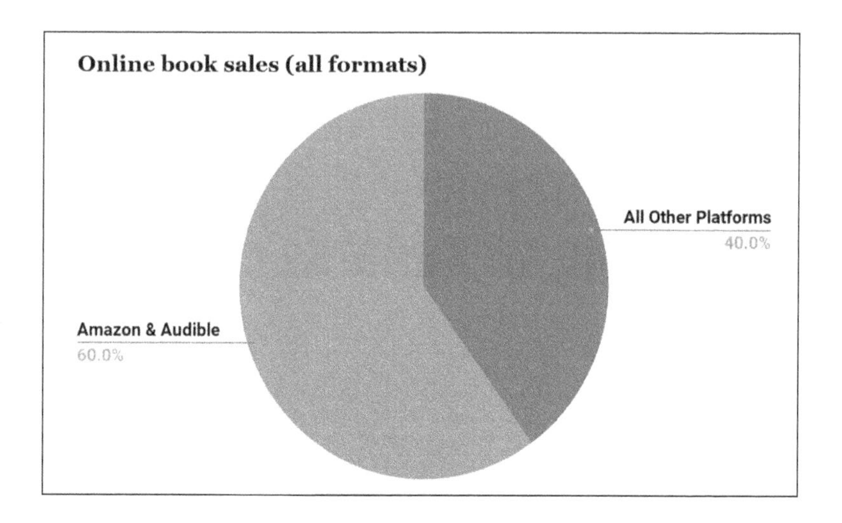

Unless you're keen on missing out on free money, you need to get your books on all these sites. It may seem like a lot of effort, complicated, and time consuming, but luckily, you have this book to make it easy for you.

There are distribution websites you can quickly and easily upload your books to, making them available for sale on literally hundreds of smaller online bookstores *and* real-world bookstores. Yes, I have seen our students' books on the shelves of airport bookstores.

We've tested many different distribution sites, and there are three that consistently generate passive book sales for us and all of our students: IngramSpark, Draft2Digital, and PublishDrive.

IngramSpark

IngramSpark is the world's second largest distributor of print books behind Amazon. Upload the print version of your books once, and that's it. You never have to think about it again.

As one of our students, Abhishek, says "Definitely publish on IngramSpark because an extra $1,000 per month is not bad for doing nothing."

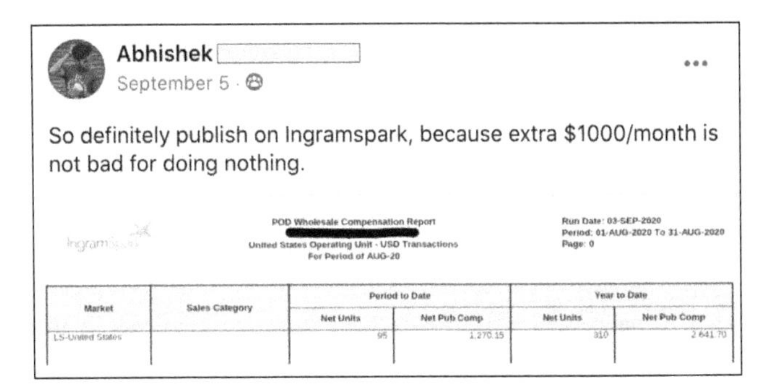

Abhishek
September 5 ·

So definitely publish on Ingramspark, because extra $1000/month is not bad for doing nothing.

POD Wholesale Compensation Report
United States Operating Unit - USD Transactions
For Period of AUG-20

Run Date: 03-SEP-2020
Period: 01-AUG-2020 To 31-AUG-2020
Page: 0

Market	Sales Category	Period to Date		Year to Date	
		Net Units	Net Pub Comp	Net Units	Net Pub Comp
LS-United States		95	1,270.15	310	2,641.70

Welcome to the world of true passive income, my friend.

Draft2Digital

Draft2Digital is similar to IngramSpark, except they will distribute the ebook version of your books to many different online book stores.

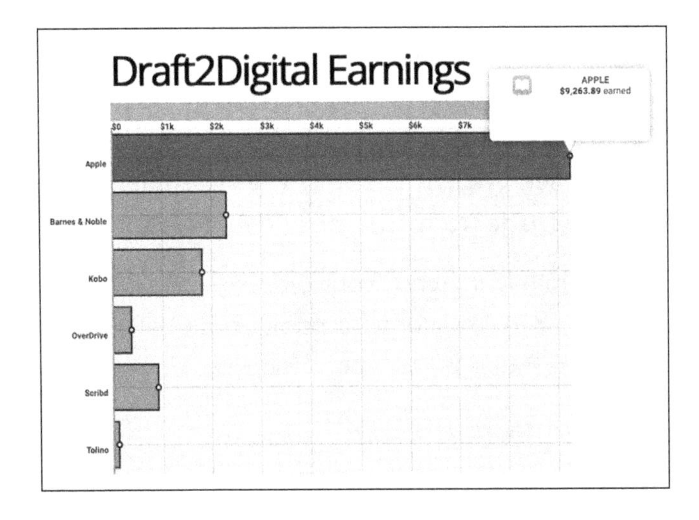

Same story here. You just upload your books, and that's it. While you won't get rich with Draft2Digital, we've still made an extra $15,000 (and counting) using their platform, and all we did was upload our books.

PublishDrive

PublishDrive is another online ebook distributor like Draft-2Digital, but they distribute to different online stores.

Once again, just upload the ebook version of your book and move on with your life.

So far, we may have only made about $8,000 with Publish-Drive, but it's the easiest $8,000 we've ever made.

I would provide the screenshots for proof, but the earnings are spread across three accounts and the dashboard doesn't allow you to sort by lifetime earnings. So you're just going to have to trust me on this one. You can picture what it looks like in your head.

That's how you create many different income streams for each book you publish. I know it's not big money, but remember that this is just us picking up the scraps and squeezing as much out of each book as possible. The vast majority of your income will be made from Amazon and Audible.

You could definitely increase your earnings on all these platforms by getting reviews for your books, but I believe your review efforts are much better spent focusing on Amazon and Audible.

31 SKIP THIS CHAPTER IF YOU HATE MONEY

Don't you wish making money was as easy as turning on a faucet? If only there were something you could simply turn on in your publishing business, and then sales would start flowing in all on their own.

Well, that does exist!

Amazon offers a cool feature where you can place your book at the very top of search results for ANY keyword you would like. As a random example, let's say you have a book that shows people how to brew their own beer at home (a surprisingly good niche). If you want your book to be shown at the very top of search results when someone searches "how to brew beer," you can do that!

What is this cool feature I'm referring to? It's Amazon Advertising.

Many people have a fear of spending money on advertising, but it's because they don't understand how valuable it is to a business. Some people believe advertising is an unnecessary expense, and they would rather use all the free methods of marketing their books. The only ones suffering from this line of thinking are you and your bank account, so hear me out before you start panicking that I'm recommending you spend money on ads for your books.

All of the biggest companies (and publishers) in the world spend A LOT of money on advertising. Why? Because it makes them EVEN MORE money. If they put $1 into advertising, they get $2 back (or more). It's that simple. James Patterson spends more money on advertising than any other publisher—and makes more!

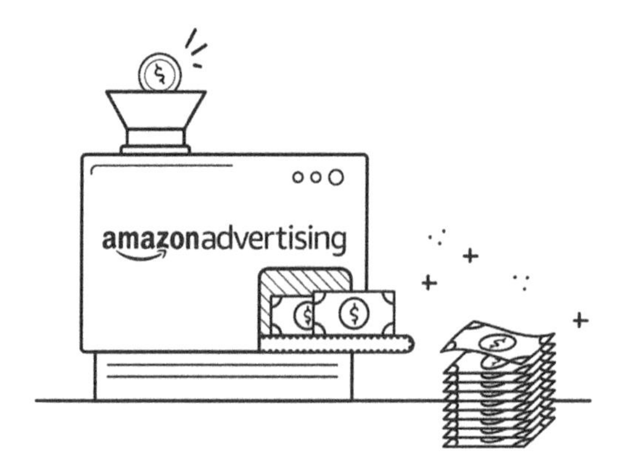

Some people fear spending money on advertising because they're worried they won't make the money back that they spend on it. Of course, you can't run ads to a bad product and expect profit. This is why it's important to have a good title, a pretty cover, and positive reviews for your book.

But what makes Amazon Advertising even easier than other platforms like Facebook Advertising is that you are only showing your book to only the most interested of customers.

When someone searches "how to brew beer" into Amazon, they already have their credit card in their hands, ready to buy a book about beer brewing. They're just trying to decide which one (or ones) to buy. That's when Amazon ads come to the rescue to make sure your book is shown.

And if someone sees your ad and doesn't click it, you don't pay a penny. You only pay when someone actually clicks on an ad for your book, at which point, there is a very high likelihood that they're buying.

Let's say you've built a nice $5,000/month income from your books and audiobooks using everything you've learned from this book so far. You can easily turn that into $10,000/month just by adding Amazon ads to your business. Even if you have to spend $3,000 to do that, you've now made $7,000 in profit in one month instead of $5,000.

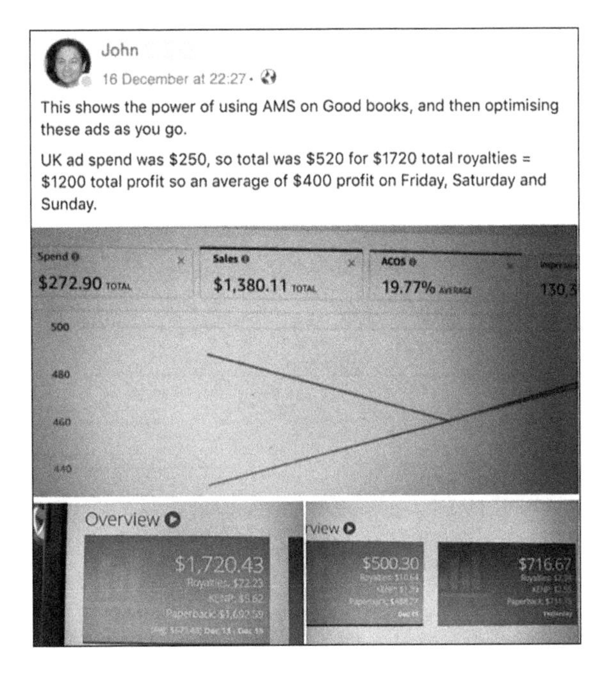

John used Amazon Ads to make $1,200 in total profit from his ebooks and print books in three days. This does not include audiobooks because, as of the time of this writing, you cannot run audiobook ads on Audible.

32

THE SECRET TO SCALE

In this chapter, I'll be revealing the secret to scaling your Amazon publishing business to over $10K per month and far beyond—if that's what you'd like to do. The secret I'll be revealing is what Soorej did to scale his Amazon publishing business to over $100,000 per month.

But first, I want to recap what we've covered so far and break it down into a simple 9-step process.

1) Pick a niche you enjoy that's proven to be profitable (look at the data).

2) Create a nice title that includes your top keywords.

3) Get a quality book written by a ghostwriter (you can use a company or a freelancer).

4) Get a good-looking book cover made by a professional.

5) Publish and gather reviews.

6) Get your book narrated into an audiobook.

7) Create bundles.

8) Multiply your income streams on platforms outside of Amazon and Audible.

9) Turn on Amazon ads.

That's how you make full-time income in this business. So how do you scale that to 6-figures a year and beyond?

Hint:
It's shocking.

Are you ready?

You repeat
the process.

I know I built up a lot of anticipation only to give such a lame answer. I'm sorry. I hope I didn't let you down, but you should be thrilled that this is what the secret is to scaling. It's not a complicated new process. You just repeat the same actions you've already done again and again until your income is at a level that you're satisfied with.

People have a way of overcomplicating things because they think success needs to be hard and complex. It doesn't. Success comes from figuring out which actions yield results (what this book is for) then rinsing and repeating.

The ones making big money in this business are not the high-IQ individuals who are always trying new strategies and methods in hopes of finding something that works even better. Those are the people who are often stuck in the same spot 12 months later because they couldn't stick to one thing consistently.

The people making big money in this *one* business are the ones who have been putting in time, effort, and focus consistently, week after week, over a longer period of time.

Take Garry, for example. He started his Amazon book publishing business four years ago. Less than a year in, he was making full-time income. Another year of consistent action later, he more than doubled his publishing income. Another two years of repeating the same actions, slowly chipping away one day at a time, and he reached his personal best of over $48,000 in one month (just from his audiobooks, by the way).

Audible, Inc.
1 Washington Park
Newark NJ 07102

Payment Advice
Jan 28, 2021

Payment Date	Payment Currency	Payment Amount	Payment Ref ID
Jan 29, 2021	USD	48,590.56	EFT-10492402

There is no top-secret strategy that the highest-earning publishers are using. They're just repeating the process that they already know works.

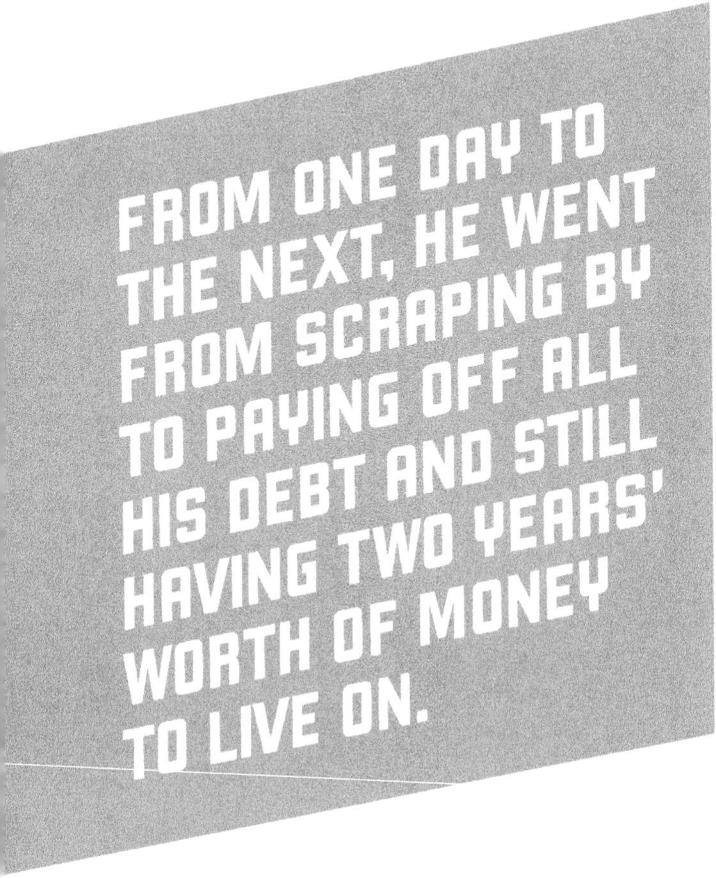

FROM ONE DAY TO THE NEXT, HE WENT FROM SCRAPING BY TO PAYING OFF ALL HIS DEBT AND STILL HAVING TWO YEARS' WORTH OF MONEY TO LIVE ON.

33

HOW TREVOR MADE OVER $100,000 IN A DAY

How's that for a sexy chapter title??

For a lot of people, $100,000 in one day sounds like a pipe dream. Even if I showed you how someone did that (which I will), you'll probably still be telling yourself, "that could never happen to me."

If that's how you feel, I'm about to show you exactly how to pull it off. After reading this chapter, not only will you agree with me that $100,000 in a day is realistic for anyone (including you), but you'll also see that it's actually undershooting it.

Trevor Somerville is the epitome of "a normal guy" (Trevor, if you're reading this, you know what I mean). He grew up in the Vancouver area, didn't do exceptionally well in school, dropped out of college, and spent his 20s jumping from job to job, trying to find one he didn't hate. He worked as a pet store manager, used car salesman, and delivery driver. He once had a cubicle job selling office supplies and a night job stocking shelves at a tire shop. He has tried almost everything.

When I asked Trevor what pushed him to eventually take action on his own business, he said, "I just realized that I'm gonna die one day. I couldn't take it anymore."

He tried and failed at many different things online before finding publishing in 2017, but it was not a smooth journey to success.

He published a bunch of random books but didn't have a clue what he was doing. While his books sold a bit every month, it wasn't anything life-changing for him.

The potential of the business was obvious to Trevor, if only he could figure out how to do it right. With a little bit of our help and a bunch of mistakes along the way, he got his publishing income just high enough to quit his job and start traveling the world.

Within six months, that catalog of random books made him over $100,000 in a single day.

You're probably thinking, "How in the world did he scale his business so fast?!" Well, he actually didn't scale his business at all.

Understand that Amazon book publishing is one of the only true passive income business models that exists online, and each book you create is an asset that produces money every month on its own.

The other common way of creating passive income would be to buy real estate, rent it out, and collect monthly rental income. That's just not an option for most people because you need A LOT of money to get started.

When you have investors analyzing an investment opportunity, whether it be in either real estate or a business, most are looking to invest in something that creates passive income. They don't want to put in work themselves; they want their money to do the work for them.

Because of this, publishing businesses are highly coveted on the open market. There are wealthy individuals all around us looking to get their hands on one and pay YOU a lot of money for it.

So that's what Trevor did. He sold his publishing business for a big, fat, 6-figure payday.

From one day to the next, he went from scraping by to paying off all his debt and still having two years' worth of money to live on. If he were to travel to Thailand or Bali and live there, that's five years of living costs covered in one nice direct deposit.

If you want to hear Trevor's entire story, we did an hour-long podcast episode with him in February 2021. Go to publishinglife.com/trevor to watch that podcast episode with video.

Trevor's publishing business wasn't particularly impressive and he would agree. A really good one can sell for multiple six figures and even seven figures easily.

So how does the selling process work?

The go-to broker that Trevor and others that have sold their publishing business used is Empire Flippers (www.empireflippers.com). They handle the entire selling process, from finding buyers, transferring ownership, receiving the payment, and everything in between.

As Trevor explains in the podcast episode, the selling process with Empire Flippers is very easy. They start by running the financials of your business to determine a listing price. They will look at your last 12 months of profit and multiply that by 30x to 40x to determine the listing price. Other factors like whether you have an email list or not and whether sales are trending up or down in recent months will determine if your valuation is closer to 30x or 40x.

So if your publishing business has made an average of just $5,000 per month profit for the last 12 months, you can sell that for $150,000 to $200,000.

Even at just $1,000 per month, you can get $30,000 to $40,000 for it all at once.

Most don't even know that their publishing business can be sold or how much they can get for it. I mentioned it to a publishing friend of ours, so he ran the numbers in his head and realized he could get around $1.7 million for his business. That's a huge number, but it also means giving up $40,000+ per month in recurring income.

Like I said earlier, publishing businesses are highly sought after because of the passive nature of them. Empire Flippers has a huge network and will connect you with 10+ interested buyers almost instantly.

If you ask me, I suggest you build your publishing business with the end goal of selling it in one to two years down the line for a life-changing amount of money. It could be enough to pay off your entire mortgage, take a couple of years off from work completely, help out your parents, or fast track your retirement.

Don't forget to go to publishinglife.com/trevor to hear Trevor's story about how publishing changed his life and how he sold his business for over $100,000.

End-of-Module Roundup

You learned that bundles (or boxsets) are an incredibly powerful strategy for increasing your publishing income just by leveraging the content you already have.

You learned that bundles essentially allow you to get three money-making books for the price of two.

You learned that Amazon and Audible are the biggest book and audiobook stores in the world, but they are not the only ones. **You want your books available for sale in as many places as possible.**

You learned that IngramSpark, Draft2Digital, and PublishDrive are great platforms you can use to distribute your books to dozens of smaller online stores. **This is how you create more income streams for each book.**

You learned that Amazon ads are an incredible tool for getting your book in front of as many people as possible. You'd only be missing out on more money if you don't use them.

You learned that there is no secret to scaling your publishing business to $20,000 per month and beyond. The ones making the most are the ones that have done this the longest. **Stick with it and repeat the process. That's the secret.**

You learned that unlike many other business models, a publishing business can be sold for a large sum. This is how Trevor made over $100,000 in one day from his publishing business.

Let's continue to Module 6, where I'll explain all the intangible 'keys to success' that we have discovered from working with over 10,000 students over the past few years.

MODULE 6

DISCOVERIES

34 THE INVISIBLE FORCE

At this point, you have all the tactical "how to" knowledge to go out there and pick a profitable niche, come up with a juicy title, get a professional book cover made, get a world-class narrator, launch your book in all formats on all platforms, and make real, literal, passive income for the rest of your life.

For a book you paid $20 or $30 for, that's some pretty insane value you've gotten.

BUT ...

You need more.

Having coached this process to over 10,000 people in the last few years, we've made quite a few discoveries along the way. One is that a lack of "how to" information is **not** what separates the winners from the losers.

I've talked to many people who just cannot seem to make this business or any other business work. While everyone has their own unique challenges, they all communicate the same over-all struggles. It's as if there is some invisible force holding them back and stopping them from putting in the work and time they know is required.

Have you ever felt that way?

I know I have. I'm feeling it right now.

This book was supposed to be finished weeks ago, yet here I am with still another five chapters to go because of this unseen diabolical force that apparently doesn't want me to finish this book!

Simply put, this invisible force is just—Life.

More specifically, that means:

- Our environment
- Other commitments
- Finances
- Disadvantages
- Health issues
- Circle of friends
- Self-doubts

This is what stops people from finding publishing success. 100 percent of the time, when someone fails, it is because they are allowing these factors to get in the way.

I am NOT saying these factors are stopping you. What I am saying is you are ALLOWING these factors to stop you.

At any given time in your life, you will always have a combination of these factors working against you. We *all* deal with

these things. Literally 8,000,000,000 (that's 8 billion) out of 8,000,000,000 of us. The difference between the winners and losers is how they react to these different factors and whether they let it stop them.

I understand it can be hard. These are not challenges that I take lightly, and that's why I'll be tackling them in this module.

This module is a collection of the most valuable lessons we have learned working with over 10,000 students. We'll be diving deep into all things that have nothing to do with publishing but everything to do with your level of success in this business.

Understand that there is always someone else out there that has been faced with the same challenging circumstances as you and has made it work. Remember Soorej? I obviously don't know your current life situation, but I have a hard time imagining that your challenges are greater than those he faced. He was a full-time student with a full-time job making $150 per month, and English was his second language. Now his publishing business makes six figures per month.

Go to Chapter 39 to see a full list of people with every disadvantage you could think of who still managed to create life-changing success with publishing.

Publishing in and of itself is very easy. It is making the commitment to prioritize it and stick with it that is hard, but it's a choice that is 100% within your control.

35 THE POWER OF ACCOUNTABILITY

To reiterate again, the step-by-step "how to" part of making money with Amazon publishing is easy. It's the simple act of taking action and sticking with it that trips people up.

The more I dug into it trying to figure out WHY people quit, I discovered that this is actually the case for almost every goal people set for themselves.

Take weight loss, for example. Boil it down to its core, and all you have to do is:

1) Consume fewer calories (eat less)

and/or

2) Burn more calories (exercise more)

That's all weight loss is. All illnesses aside, it is simple and clear what actions you need to take, yet so many people still fail to lose weight. Why?

If you've ever tried to lose weight, you probably started your weight loss journey and realized that wasn't the hard part. On Day 1, motivation is always sky-high, so getting your butt out of bed to go to the gym at 7 a.m. is a piece of cake. Your epic workout fuels you even more, so you whip up some egg whites and spinach for breakfast. You CRUSHED Day 1.

As the week continues, you feel little temptations popping up here and there, but you are riding high on motivation and are dedicated to making a change. You say NO to all of them.

The weekend comes around, and you get invited to hang out with friends and family. Since none of your friends or family are on the weight loss journey with you, there are snacks everywhere. You tell yourself, "I've had a good week. I deserve a treat."

With a little encouragement from your friends who are enjoying delicious food all around you, that turns into a second treat, and a third one. Now you feel like everything you worked so hard for during the week went to waste and all that motivation you felt during the week is close to gone.

From there, it slowly unravels, and within weeks, you're back into the same eating and exercise habits you had before.

It's a dangerous cycle that I'm sure everyone has been through in one way or another.

The hard part when trying to achieve anything isn't getting started. It's consistently continuing to work toward your goal even when life gets in the way.

So how do you fix this? It's easy for me to say, "Just build the discipline and strength to say no to all temptations," but that's hard. I can't do that either.

The one thing I started doing that made not giving up infinitely easier was by doing it with someone else that shared the same goals and ambition as myself.

It's having people around you (in real life or online) to encourage you, keep you accountable, and make sure you're taking the actions that are required to be successful.

For Christian and myself, having each other was the biggest blessing in the world.

When we first started with Amazon publishing back in 2016, we both had so much pent-up energy and ambition. We were so motivated to be successful that taking the first action and "starting" was never a problem.

But as exciting as any new venture is right when you start it, that excitement and motivation will always slowly begin to fade over time. When that intense fire inside you diminishes just a little bit, you start to get sloppy, and you let little things slide. Now you're snoozing on the alarm clock, watching a bit more TV than you should, and searching for good reasons to procrastinate.

When you're going at it alone and you slack on your goals, the only person you're hurting is yourself. I've found that I don't really mind letting myself down because I do it all the time. But when I know that me slacking isn't only hurting me, it's hurting Christian and letting him down too—*that* sucks.

We would work independently on our own publishing businesses, so at the end of each day, we would check in with each other and share what we worked on, what we struggled with that day, and our biggest win of the day (we still do this now). This kept us going at a high pace every day.

Every time Christian or I caught the other one starting to slip up, we would point it out immediately. That kind of accountability is what made all the difference.

Let's use a personal trainer as an example. What is the real benefit of having one? Are they finally revealing all the secrets to weight loss you never knew about? Do they know all the best exercises that you otherwise could never figure out on your own? Of course not.

The benefit of working with a personal trainer is that they make you show up to the gym, and they keep you showing up consistently over and over because that's what it takes to get real results. They're not really doing anything special, they're just there to keep you accountable and on track.

So in the context of a publishing business, what's the best way of doing that?

- Find a friend/spouse/family member to do this with you
- Join a mastermind
- Make friends in a community of publishers

Is this required for success? No, of course not. But if you know you're the kind of person that has a hard time sticking to things or is lazy or gives up easily, this will make everything infinitely easier for you. I promise you. And why not make things as easy as we can?

When we first started publishing, one of the first things we did was ingrain ourselves into an online community of other publishers with the same ambition and goal to make $10,000 per month and create complete freedom in our lives.

Others would share their progress and success, which always boosted my motivation and energy levels every time I felt it starting to dip. Now that I think about it, more than 50 percent of my closest friends today came from that first publishing community we joined in 2016. Many of them we've met up with all across the world, and we are now friends for life. Ollie El-Gorr, who wrote the foreword to this book, is someone we met in that online publishing community.

So I advise you, don't go at this completely alone. The statistics say that, simply due to human nature, you are likely to give up at some point along the way. All the success stories you've seen in this book are the ones that pushed through even when motivation started to fade and unexpected bumps in the road came up.

If you just stay committed and don't give up, you can completely change your life in less than 12 months, no matter where you're starting from. Finding a like-minded community will make that part so much easier.

PUBLISHING SUCCESS COMES AT A COST, BUT THE REWARD IS GREATER THAN ANYTHING ELSE ON THIS GREEN EARTH.

36

HOW TO KNOW IF YOU WILL BE SUCCESSFUL

They say you can tell a lot about a person just by listening to the kinds of questions they ask, and that's especially true when it comes to business.

I would go so far as to say that I can even predict whether someone will be making a full-time income from their publishing business or back at their 9–5 job in the next 12 months based only on the intial questions they ask.

If someone asks either of these questions, it's a huge red flag that their mindset needs some work to be a successful publisher/entrepreneur.

"How fast can I make $10,000 per month?"

While there is nothing unequivocally wrong with wanting to make as much money as fast as possible (don't we all?), it's a problem if that's what drives your decision making.

In the normal working world, you get paid by the hour. Literally, all you have to do is show up, and you will start earning money instantly. No matter if your work is low or high quality, you're guaranteed to get paid.

This is what someone who has been an employee their entire life is used to, and therefore they often carry this expectation over into publishing.

They'll put in time and effort for a couple of months, and if they haven't made any money yet, their first reaction is: "I've been working at this for two months and still haven't made money, I could have been working at my job and made more money this whole time. What a waste of time. I'm done."

The truth is that with any business, there's a delay. It takes time before you can reap the rewards of the work and time you put in, no matter what entrepreneurial endeavor you get into. So this expectation of "fast money" needs to go because it isn't happening. First, you put in your time and effort, then you get rewarded for that work months down the line.

I've also noticed that the ones who want to make money the fastest are always the ones to quit the fastest. If they don't see a quick enough return, they move on to the next shiny business model, hoping that will make a faster return (it never does).

I run into these types all the time. They'll say, "Hey, I've started a bunch of online businesses in the last few years, but none of it worked. How do I know publishing will be any different?"

Let me tell you. It won't be any different. These are the same people asking, "How fast can I make $10,000 per month?"

While we're on the topic, let's answer the question now, so I don't have to deal with it later.

Instead of just saying "it depends," which is the honest answer, I'll give you a range of how fast others have been able to achieve it.

The quickest students of ours that I'm aware of are Dane, who went 0 to $10,000 per month in six months, and Daniel, who went from $0 to $12,000 per month—also in six months. Funny enough, Daniel is now one of many coaches in our program and does one-on-one coaching and group coaching for our students.

Some others take two to three years to reach that milestone. It's funny how I say "two to three years" as if it's a long time, but if we compare that to the time it takes to go through college and work your way up to a $10,000 per month job, you're looking at 6–8 years if everything goes according to plan (while collecting a massive amount of debt along the way). Truthfully, most career paths never have a good chance of ever reaching a $10,000/month income. With publishing, there's nothing stopping you from growing to $20k, $30k a month and beyond.

Christian hit $10,000 per month for the first time in his publishing business after 14 months, and that included many obstacles, mistakes, and failures along the way.

Moving on to the next red-flag question, indicating your mindset isn't yet in the right place to be a successful publisher/entrepreneur: *"Where can I find the cheapest writers, designers, narrators?"*

If you're making decisions in your business based on "What's the cheapest," you're starving yourself of the opportunity to make much more money in the future.

That's what we call, "Stepping over dollars to pick up pennies."

What you're doing is you're trying to save a penny now, but as a result, you're missing out on making a dollar (or many dollars) in the future.

To put this in publishing context ... Let's say you want to save as much money as possible when creating a book. So you decide you're going to go with the cheapest ghostwriting company, make a short book, find a $10 cover designer on Fiverr and a $20 PFH narrator.

This will get you a complete ebook, print book, and audiobook ready to publish for about $180.

A crappy little thing like this probably won't make more than $30–$40 a month.

On the contrary, if you were making your decisions based on "How do I create a book that people want to buy," you're looking at spending maybe $1,000.

A book like this should be making $300 a month easily with the potential for thousands EVERY month.

To make this abundantly obvious, take a look at the chart below. Theoretically, Book 1 earns $50 per month and Book 2 earns only $200. This would be considered high earnings for a low-quality book and very low earnings for a high-quality book, but I just want to prove my point.

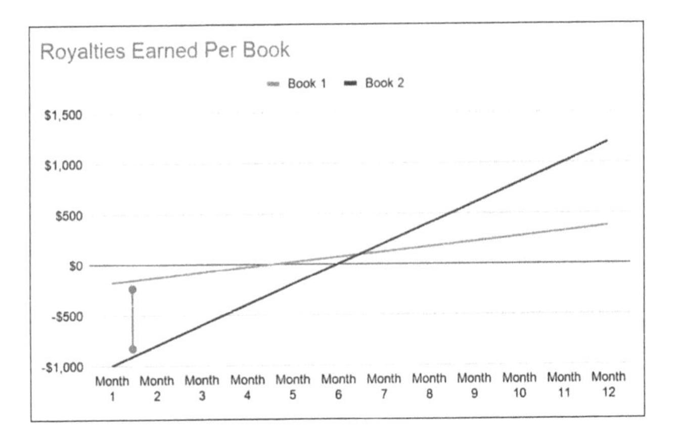

With Book 1, you are only saving hundreds of dollars in the short run. Even if it takes you two to three months longer to recoup your investment, your long-term earnings opportunity with Book 2 is enormous compared to Book 1.

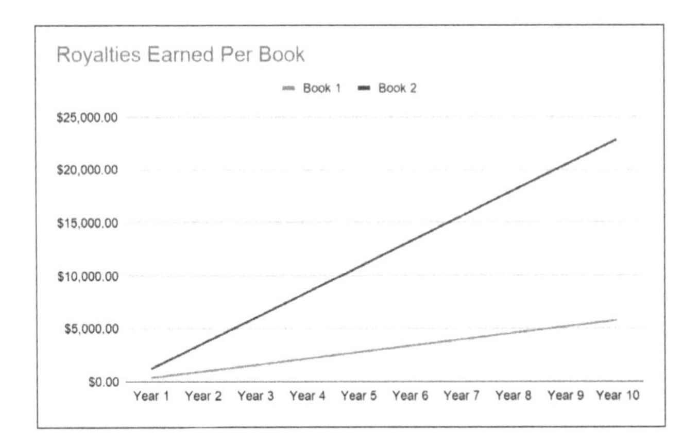

We're talking a difference of tens of thousands of dollars over the course of 10 years and beyond. Many are too focused on saving costs now, not understanding that it's killing their long-term earnings.

As I've said, many have trouble thinking more than a couple of months into the future, but I promise you, 12 months from now WILL come no matter what, and when it does, you'll be thanking yourself. Ten years from now, which I can guarantee you will also come, and when it does, your books will STILL be out and making money.

Don't try cutting corners to save a little money now because it will cost you big in the future.

I understand that some people are limited financially, but don't let that impact the quality of work that goes into your books.

Instead, work more hours at your job and lower your living expenses. As much as you might not want to do that, it's simply a part of the process. I don't know anyone successful that hasn't been through that.

Publishing and entrepreneurship as a whole is an investment today for a better tomorrow. Write that on a piece of paper and place it on your fridge as a reminder to yourself every day because sometimes there will be times where you feel like you're putting in more time and effort than you're getting out. That's when the thoughts of quitting start to float around in your head, but as long as you understand that publishing and any business success takes time, you'll be fine.

This may sound harsh, but if you can't accept that fact, then you don't deserve to reap the same rewards as us. Publishing success comes at a cost, but the reward is greater than anything else on this green earth. If you want fast money with no serious investment, then you're better off with a job.

> "If you don't find a way to make money while you sleep, you will work until you die."
>
> —Warren Buffet

37

HOW MANY DO I NEED TO MAKE $10,000 PER MONTH?

If for some reason, you've ever wondered which question we get asked more than any other, this is it. That's why I want to dedicate a whole chapter to answering this question loud and clear in full detail with explanations, so we don't have to repeat ourselves anymore.

So how many books do you need to make $10K per month?

The honest answer is ... It depends.

I know that's not what you want to hear, but rest assured, I will give you a ballpark number later in the chapter. But the truth is, I can't tell you how many books you will have to publish before you hit $10,000 per month because it depends on several factors.

It depends on the demand/competition of your niche, your book title, your cover, how many reviews your books have, whether you created book bundles or not, whether you published your book in all formats and on all platforms or not, whether you're running Amazon ads or not. It depends on if and how well you execute the steps I have laid out in this book.

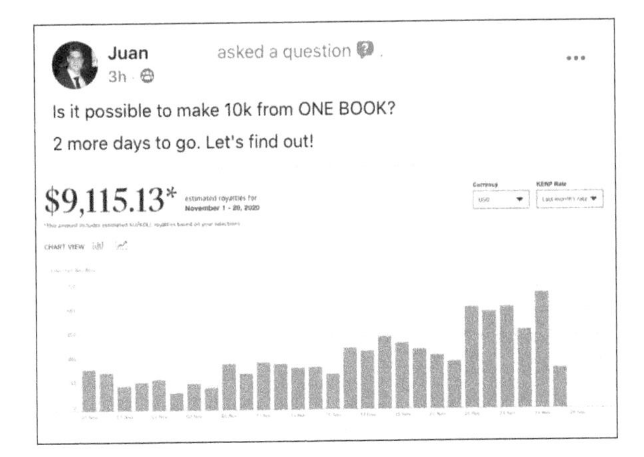

Here is Juan, who made over $10,000 in one month from one book.

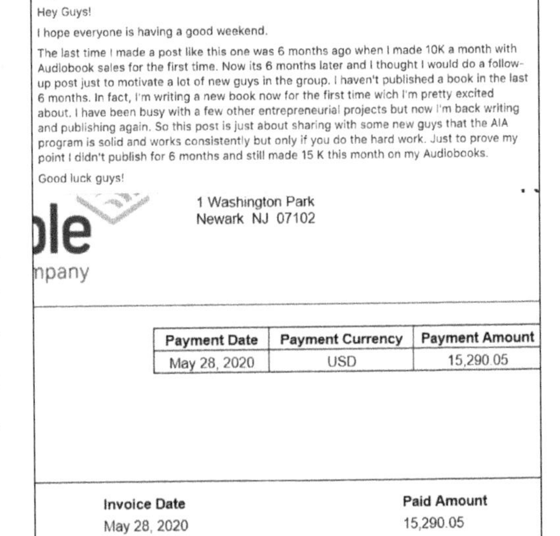

Here is Hennie, who made $15,000 in one month with seven books.

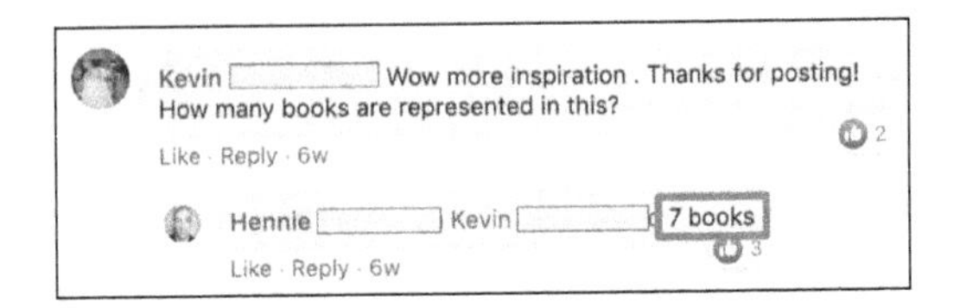

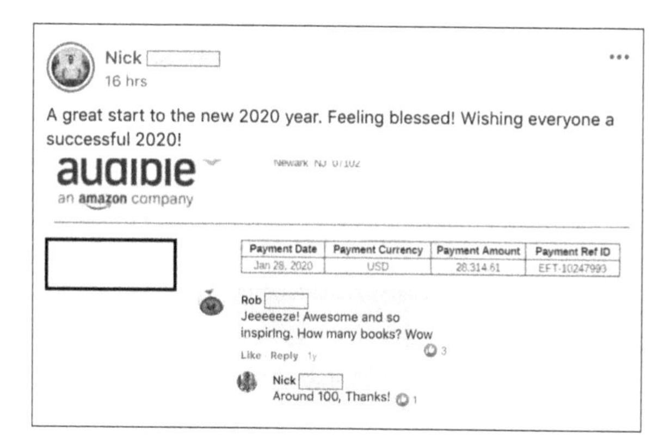

Here is Nick, who made $28,000 in one month with 100 books.

That's a pretty wide range. But if you're going to force me to put a ballpark number on how many books it takes to make $10,000 per month, it's this ...

Five.

Just five books. That is very attainable as long as you focus on each step and do them well.

"More Books = More Money" is a very poor way of viewing this business because, although there is some truth to that statement, that mindset will have you rushing through the steps just to get more books out.

Take your time, do the fundamentals well, focus on hitting at least 100 reviews during your book launch, and apply all the income multiplying techniques covered in Module 5.

If you quickly throw five low-quality books together and just publish them without getting any reviews and you expect sales to start flying in at a $10,000 per month level, you are sorely mistaken. That would be incredibly unreasonable to expect.

It's funny how people hate on the "get rich quick" schemes and then are disappointed when they learn a business actually requires some effort and commitment. Sorry!

I know this is a cliche quote, but I cannot explain it any simpler than this: "What you put in is what you get out." If you want more out, you have to put more time and effort in.

38

HOW TO SHORTCUT SUCCESS

Earlier in the book, I mentioned a student of ours, Dane, who flipped his entire life around by going from $0 to $10,000 per month in his publishing business in just six months. Not long after, he hit nearly $20,000 in one month.

Dane
Visual storyteller · 1 June

After getting my Earnings Report the other day, April officially marks the biggest month for my publishing business to date.

I remember my first royalty payment back in September of last year being around $700 USD... If I would've told myself I'd be making close to $20k in a month in 7 months time, I definitely wouldn't have believed a single word coming out of my mouth lol.

I can't wait to see what happen over the next 7 months, thank you to Rasmus Mikkelsen Christian Mikkelsen and everyone else who have helped me get to this stage 🔥

He committed fully to the business from day one, and all the credit goes to him for making it happen, but the truth is ... He had a shortcut.

A shortcut that allowed him to skip the hardest part of starting any new business for the first time.

Dane was not our typical publishing student. In fact, we never even explained to him what publishing was until months after we met in person.

Let me explain ...

In the fall of 2018, we were looking to hire someone to help us film and edit videos for our YouTube channel. We put up a post on our Instagram page to see if anyone was interested in being flown to Bali and then traveling with us as our videographer.

For Dane, this was the perfect opportunity to leave his hometown near Vancouver, Canada, quit his low-paying job, start traveling, and improve as a videographer. So he sent us a message, we hopped on a call, and less than a month later, he was with us in Bali, shooting and editing videos for us.

He literally lived with us in our villa in Bali.

It wasn't until about six months later, when Dane had some free time, that we all agreed it was a good idea to get him into publishing to make some additional side money.

He saw our results and all our students' results firsthand, which gave him insane amounts of confidence that he could really make it happen if he committed to this.

At that point, we essentially became his publishing mentors. We had 24/7 oversight of all the work he was doing and all the books he was publishing.

Everything we knew up to that point had been accumulated over three years of publishing many books and wasting a lot of time and money experimenting with different publishing strategies that didn't work. We tried publishing books of different lengths, different languages, all the ghostwriting services out there, and almost every niche you can think of.

Let me tell you that we made a lot of mistakes along the way. Like A LOT A LOT. We paid the price for those mistakes in the form of valuable time and money, but that's the process of trying to figure out anything new without guidance. We could never have the success we have today without all the mistakes we made in the past.

Now Dane had access to all this wealth of knowledge and experience, only he didn't have to go through the same struggles to gain it. We passed along all the learning lessons and strategies that worked, and he was able to apply them from day one.

A friend of mine recently said this to me, and it has now become one of my favorite quotes.

"A smart man learns from his mistakes, a wise man learns from the mistakes of others."

That's how Dane shortcut his way to success and hit his first $10,000 month only six months later.

Dane
Visual storyteller · 1 January at 11:07

My goal back in August when I first started publishing was by December this year to make $5k USD in 1 month.

December: $6776.99 (KDP) $3572.30 (ACX)
Total: $10,349.29 ***(13462.87 CAD)***

It seriously blows me away.

Hopefully this post can give some of you hope and seriously prove to you that not only KDP can make you a bunch of money, but publishing itself is something special.

If you compare that to where I was six months into my publishing journey ...

I was busy publishing a series of crime thriller fiction novels called *Hardline* under the pen name R.M. Galloway. Yep, that's one of my failed publishing experiments. It would have been nice if I had someone to tell me, "THIS IS A STUPID IDEA." That would have saved about six months of my time.

That experience taught me to never try something new without the guidance of an expert. It's honestly a cheat code and far and away the fastest and easiest way to shortcut your way to success.

If I had to learn something new and couldn't find the best and learn from them, I would be LOST. There is no way I would ever put in the time and effort to figure out how to do something when I can just go directly to someone that has already figured it out. They will tell me exactly what to do and how to do it, so I can cut my learning curve in half and rapidly accelerate my results.

For example, this is my first time writing a full-length book myself. I have no previous book writing experience, nor was I magically born with the ability to write a book like this. So what did I do? I sought out an expert and then paid him $30,000 to show me how to write this book.

Some will say, "Oh my God, what a waste of money!"

But the truth is... I would waste much more time and money through the mistakes I make than the cost of that coaching. That's not even considering how much more money I'll make due to getting that expert guidance. Just the mistakes I would have made would directly add up to more money wasted than the cost of that training.

That's a $30,000 investment upfront, but it immediately saves me six months (probably more) of learning and will directly pay me back 100x in the future.

Look at any successful entrepreneur. They all had guidance from someone that came before them. I cannot stress the life-changing value of learning personally from someone who has already achieved the results you want. They've made all the mistakes, and they've figured out what does and doesn't work.

So if you're at a place in your life where you're not satisfied with your job, or you're not making as much money as you want, or you just don't have the freedom to actually enjoy your life, then you have to do something about it. You will never achieve the lifestyle you want by sitting back and waiting for it to happen on its own.

How to Get More Help ...

Until 2021, our publishing program Audiobook Income Academy consisted of step-by-step video training, weekly group coaching, and an amazing community.

While this version of the program was enough to change the lives of many (see the next chapter), the experience with Dane was eye-opening. It showed me how much of a difference it can make when you have an expert there with you every step of the way.

We want to give you that same coaching experience, which is why we've hired many of our most successful students as coaches to work with people like you on a personal 1-on-1 coaching basis.

We have, by far, the biggest and most experienced team of publishing coaches in the world and all of them are past students of ours who have made publishing their full-time income.

If you'd like to learn more and see how us and our team of coaches can personally help you, go to publishinglife.com/learnmore.

Can you create a massively successful Amazon publishing business without our help?

YES, you absolutely can.

If you resort to doing this on your own, you have the information in this book and all the bonus resources included within it. We have had people achieve life-changing success just by using what they've learned from our free resources, but 99% of them come directly from our program.

Remember:

> "A smart man learns from his mistakes; a wise man learns from the mistakes of others."

39 INSPIRING SUCCESS STORIES

As I've mentioned many times, the "how-to" side of Amazon book publishing isn't challenging once you know what to do. The most important part of our job is keeping people motivated, committed, focused on their business, and consistently chipping away at it every week, even when life gets in the way.

Our students say that seeing the success of others motivates them more than anything else. So if you ever feel demotivated or tempted to procrastinate and need an instant spark of energy, open up this book, and flip to this chapter.

Here is a very short list of people who have quit their jobs and achieved life-changing results with Amazon and Audible publishing.

Out of respect to all these individuals, I will only be including their first names. We've had multiple people complain that random people message them on Facebook and Instagram, so please respect their privacy and do not message them to hear their thoughts about us or our program. Everything you see here is real.

Gerald is a young man from Peru. We actually met in person in 2018 at a live publishing mastermind event. He didn't have any money for a hotel room, so Christian and I let him sleep in our room for the two nights at the event. When we returned home from that event, he committed himself to publishing and he's now been making $10K+ per month ever since.

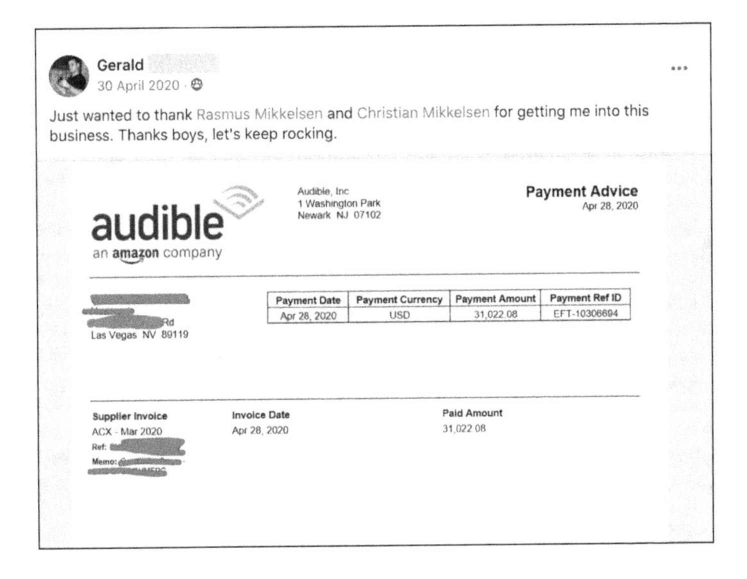

We first met **Dane** from Vancouver, Canada, when he applied to be our videographer when we were living in Bali. We video chatted, hit it off, and a month later he was living in our home in Bali filming and editing YouTube videos for us. He started publishing in his off time, then went full time into publishing when he saw the potential of it. He went from $0 to $10,000 in a month in just six months. Read his full story in Chapter 38.

Dane
Visual storyteller · 1 January at 11:07

My goal back in August when I first started publishing was by December this year to make $5k USD in 1 month.

December: $6776.99 (KDP) $3572.30 (ACX)

Total: $10,349.29 ***(13462.87 CAD)***

It seriously blows me away.

Hopefully this post can give some of you hope and seriously prove to you that not only KDP can make you a bunch of money, but publishing itself is something special.

Limon comes from Bangladesh where the average salary is about $350 per month.[8] Within a year of starting his publishing business, he was awarded the 10K Award for reaching $10,000 in one month, a very impressive income where he comes from.

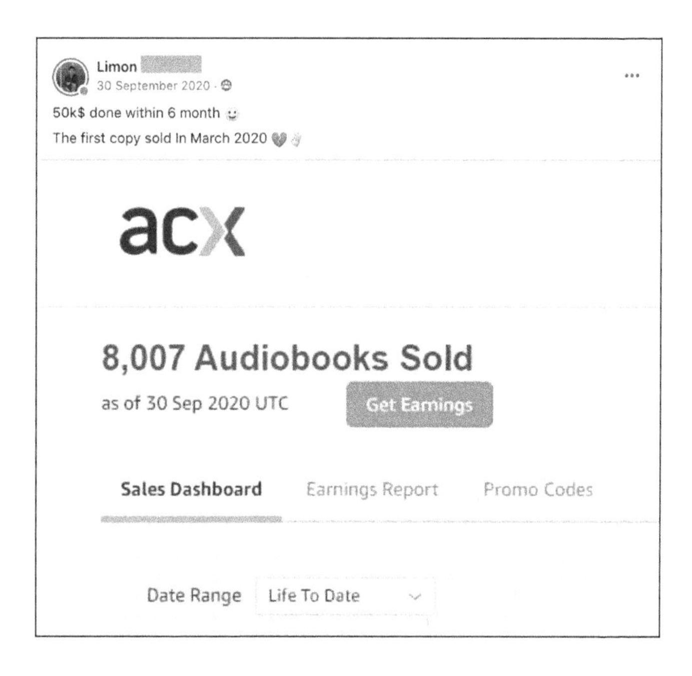

8 "Average Salary in Bangladesh 2021," The Complete Guide, accessed June 5, 2021, http://www.salaryexplorer.com/salary-survey.php?loc=18&loctype=1.

Trevor spent his whole life working different jobs he hated. He tried many different businesses such as blogging and affiliate marketing prior to finding self-publishing. Over the course of 2019, he scaled his publishing business to six figures and was able to quit his job in November 2019, and move to Bali, Indonesia. He now travels all over the world, currently living in Honolulu, Hawaii. He says it feels good to make twice as much as his boss ever did at his old job while having the freedom to live wherever he pleases. He recently sold his publishing business for six figures. Read his full story in Chapter 33.

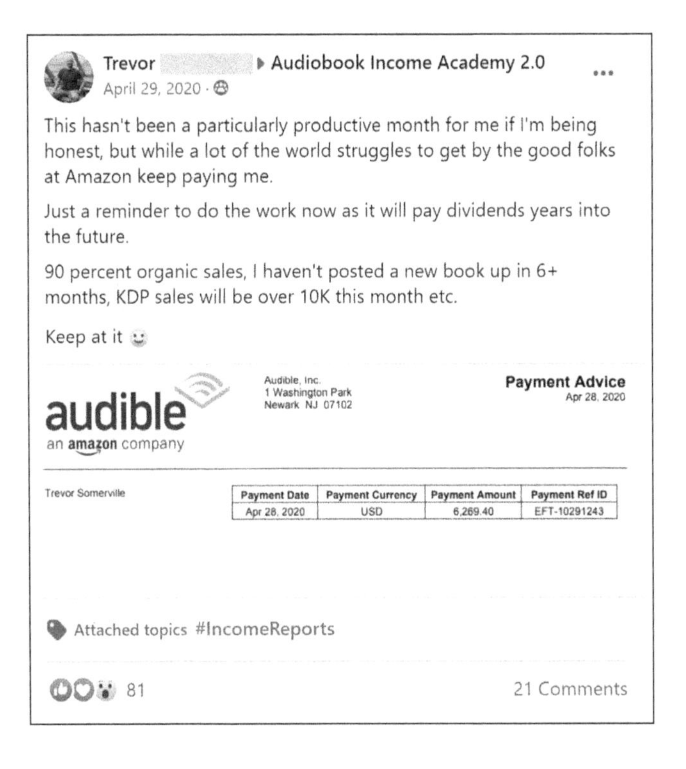

Trevor ▸ Audiobook Income Academy 2.0
April 29, 2020 ·

This hasn't been a particularly productive month for me if I'm being honest, but while a lot of the world struggles to get by the good folks at Amazon keep paying me.

Just a reminder to do the work now as it will pay dividends years into the future.

90 percent organic sales, I haven't posted a new book up in 6+ months, KDP sales will be over 10K this month etc.

Keep at it

audible
an amazon company

Audible, Inc.
1 Washington Park
Newark NJ 07102

Payment Advice
Apr 28, 2020

Trevor Somerville

Payment Date	Payment Currency	Payment Amount	Payment Ref ID
Apr 28, 2020	USD	6,269.40	EFT-10291243

Attached topics #IncomeReports

81

21 Comments

Ed was one of the first members to join AIA back in 2018. By the end of January 2019, he was averaging $50 per day in profit just as a side business, which is when he decided to go all in on publishing. Since then, he has built a sustainable publishing business that's let him quit his job, pay off all his debt, and save for a house with his wife.

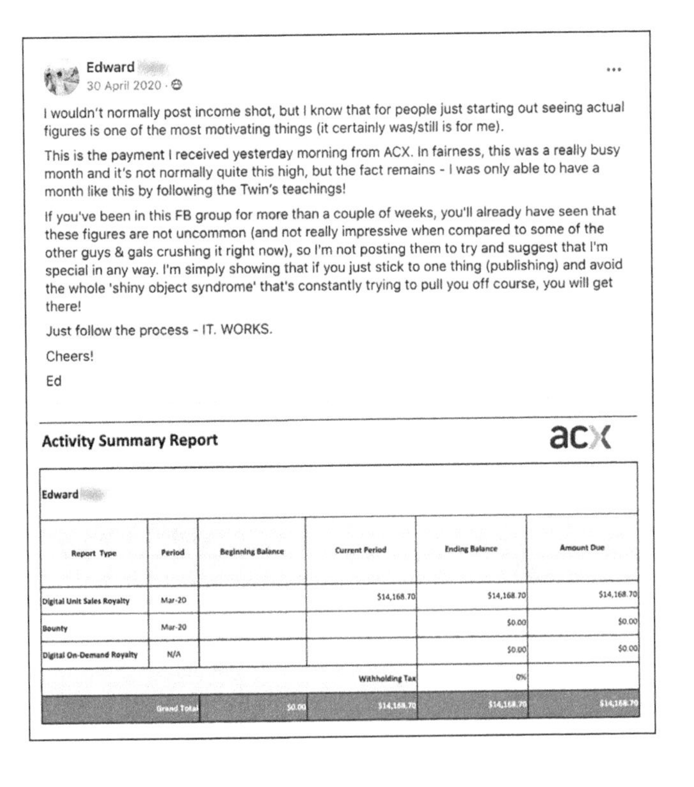

Edward
30 April 2020

I wouldn't normally post income shot, but I know that for people just starting out seeing actual figures is one of the most motivating things (it certainly was/still is for me).

This is the payment I received yesterday morning from ACX. In fairness, this was a really busy month and it's not normally quite this high, but the fact remains - I was only able to have a month like this by following the Twin's teachings!

If you've been in this FB group for more than a couple of weeks, you'll already have seen that these figures are not uncommon (and not really impressive when compared to some of the other guys & gals crushing it right now), so I'm not posting them to try and suggest that I'm special in any way. I'm simply showing that if you just stick to one thing (publishing) and avoid the whole 'shiny object syndrome' that's constantly trying to pull you off course, you will get there!

Just follow the process - IT. WORKS.

Cheers!

Ed

Activity Summary Report acx

Edward

Report Type	Period	Beginning Balance	Current Period	Ending Balance	Amount Due
Digital Unit Sales Royalty	Mar-20		$14,168.70	$14,168.70	$14,168.70
Bounty	Mar-20			$0.00	$0.00
Digital On-Demand Royalty	N/A			$0.00	$0.00
			Withholding Tax	0%	
	Grand Total	$0.00	$14,168.70	$14,168.70	$14,168.70

Now a coach in AIA, **Ivan** has worked a demanding full-time job for many years along with being married and raising two kids. While his job paid well, he wanted more free time to spend with his family. Now being a few years into his publishing journey, he recently hit a new personal record—over $15,000 in one month.

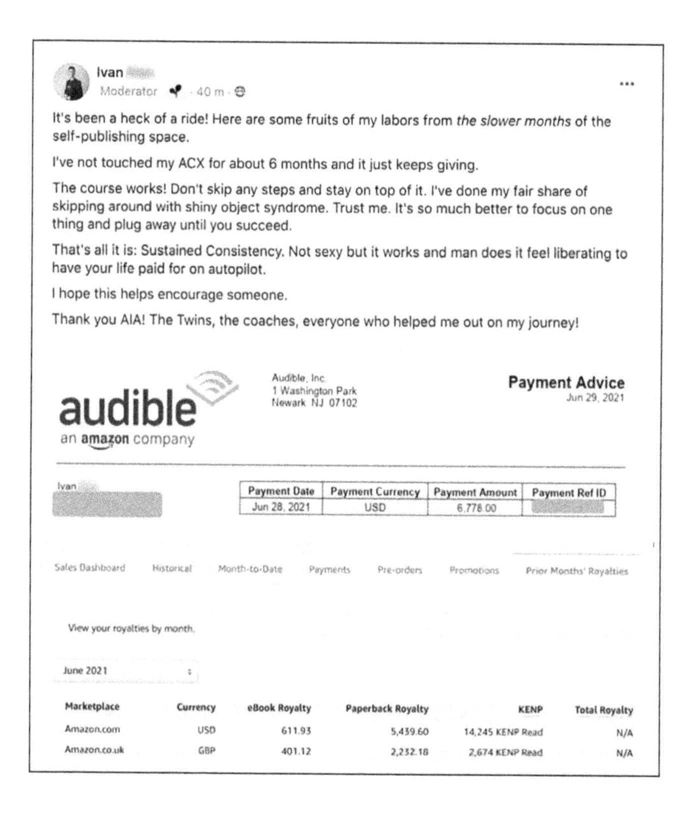

Marketplace	Currency	eBook Royalty	Paperback Royalty	KENP	Total Royalty
Amazon.com	USD	611.93	5,439.60	14,245 KENP Read	N/A
Amazon.co.uk	GBP	401.12	2,232.18	2,674 KENP Read	N/A

Cody (also a coach in AIA) has a full-time job, he's in the military, he's a public speaking coach, and he has a wife and two kids. He is a busy man to say the least, but he was still able to grow his publishing business to a full-time income even as a side hustle.

Juan (whose second language is English) was working a corporate day job for 19 years, but always dreamed of living a life where he did not need to ask his boss for permission to take a vacation. At 44 years old, he realized the only risk is doing nothing because he knew he would never be happy at his job. So he started his publishing business which he calls "one of the best decisions of my life" because it has given him complete freedom to live life how he wants. He recently sold his publishing for a multi six-figure sum.

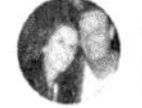

Juan Born
21 October at 00:55 ·

Today I passed a virtual milestone. More than 20.000 audiobooks sold from my ACX Account.

It´s just a number, but when I started 2 years ago, I couldn´t imagine seeing these numbers on my own account...

I hope it inspires and motivates you. Keep going and belief you can do it as well.

20,074 Total Units Sold *

as of 21 Oct 2020 UTC View Sales Dashboard

Destiny had previously failed at affiliate marketing, apps, a blog, Clickbank, and different niche sites before she finally found publishing. Now, with a publishing business paying her consistent royalties month after month, Destiny has spent the last couple of years traveling the world. She visited Thailand, Bali, Singapore, and six other countries all without even publishing a book for seven months.

Patrick holds the AIA record for greatest audiobook earnings in one month at $91,731. He says, "I have now sold close to 130,000 audiobooks on Audible—all thanks to the twins." He has a very compelling story about how he got a big start with online business about 15 years ago, went through many struggles to where he couldn't even afford a flight back home to New York, and then his life turned around when he found publishing. Read his full story in Chapter 7.

Aaminah has sold thousands of copies of her first book which became a bestseller on Amazon. She's even used it to launch her own online course which made over £4,000 in two weeks.

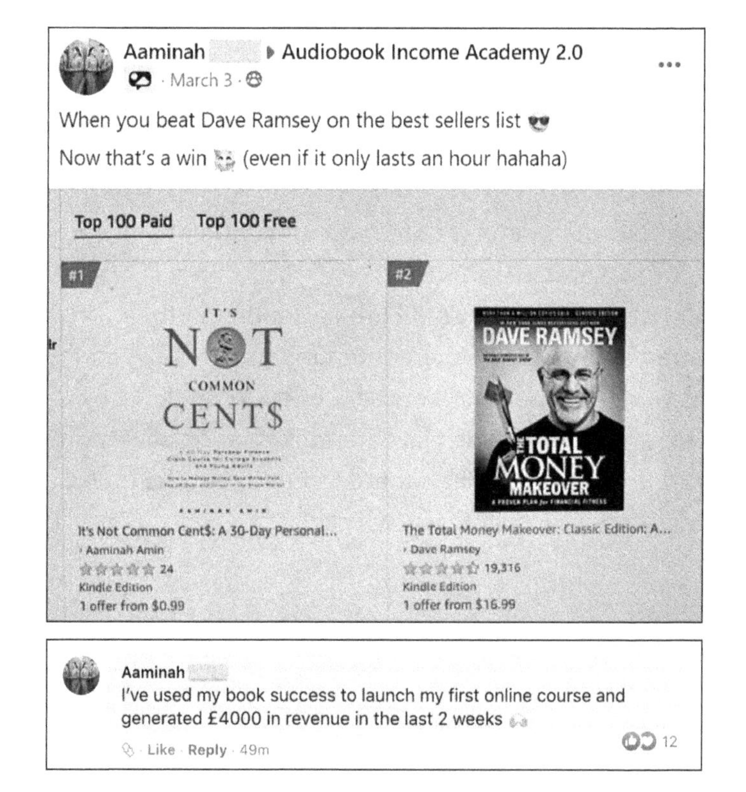

John is a young lad from the UK whose life has been completely transformed by book publishing. His publishing business is at a multi six-figure level and he has also made friends for life through the AIA community.

Arnaud from France joined AIA on the first day it was released. He loves to travel, which is why the publishing business model was a perfect fit for his adventurous lifestyle. He has sold over 50,000 audiobooks so far and will continue making passive income from his books every month for many years.

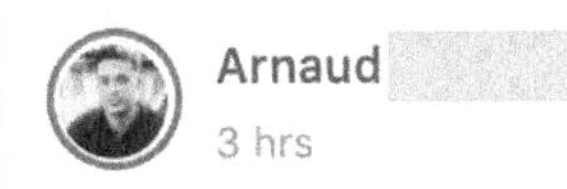

Started back in end 2018 when AIA 1.0 just launched, and have been working consistently ever since. This month (almost exactly 2 years later) I hit the 50,000 audiobook sold. Next milestone 100k!! 🚀🚀🚀

Kim is a young woman in her early 20s from Germany. She quickly realized that she was not happy working at any of her jobs. With no college degree, she started exploring entrepreneurial opportunities online and found publishing. She actually publishes books in German, and her best book has made over $20,000 profit in the last nine months.

This screenshot is of the Royalties my best book has made over the past 9 months. Subtract the ad spend from those royalties and that leaves me with 20,463.47€ (roughly $24,600) pure profit from one single book within 9 months.

This book has now over 300 reviews of which about 250 are completely organic meaning I didn't do a thing to get them and they are by real customers.

Sounds amazing? Well it is!
But truth be told, this wasn't my first book. It wasn't even my second. It was my 8th.

How did my other books do before that one?
Some did okay and brought my up to 1000€ a month while others failed miserably.

And that's okay.

As with any business you need to fail, you need to learn from mistakes and you have to push through the dip in order to grow and eventually thrive!

I could tell you so many things right now of what I did and didn't do to succeed in publishing but honestly, it's all in the course.

So I tell you this instead: All you need to succeed in publishing or any business for that matter is commitment and the will to make it work!
That's all it takes. Because if you have those two things you will not quit until you make it work!

If you're not there yet, keep going until you are and then go even further, because you are capable of BIG things!

Richard from Virginia is married, raising four kids, and has a demanding full-time job. Christian and I (Rasmus) actually met up for lunch with Richard and his wife in Virginia (we were coincidentally there on vacation with our family). Richard mentioned that he had very little time to work on publishing, but he was determined to do anything to make it work. He took action on some things we talked about during lunch and within a few months started making $4,000–$5,000 per month from those books. Years later, those books still generate really good income every month, and it's 100% passive for him.

Charlotte, Christian's wife, was introduced to publishing when we first met her on a hike in Maui in 2018 (you can go back and read the story of how we met in the introduction to this book). She loved to travel and was inspired by the lifestyle Christian and I had created for ourselves. Within a year, she had quit her job due to the money she was making from her publishing business. We have traveled all over the world together with her and although she hasn't published a book in two years, she still gets paid $1000+ per month on autopilot.

Charlotte
30 January

Lol. It's been over a year since I last published a book and every single month, like clockwork I get a email notification for $$$ in my bank account.

It's been consistently for the last six months at least $1,500 in Audible payments, plus my KDP payments which add a couple hundred as well.

Free money!

Payment Date	Payment Currency	Payment Amount
Jan 29, 2021	USD	1,512.08

Payment Date	Payment Currency	Payment Amount	P
Dec 22, 2020	USD	1,497.95	I

Payment Date	Payment Currency	Payment Amount	Pa
Nov 30, 2020	USD	1,607.18	El

Ollie is not only one of our best friends but also one of our best publishing success stories. We met back in 2017 from a random Facebook group. He started to find success with publishing and then we met in person for the first time in 2018 in Cancun. He went on to sell that publishing business for six figures and then started a new one which he scaled from $0 to $50,000 in one month in just 10 months. He has big plans to take his business to much greater heights over the coming years, and we know that he will. Congrats, Ollie. And thanks for writing our foreword!

Ollie

+2 · April 30 ·

This is my new publishing business, so the first book went live in June 2020.

Some advice for the newbies in here
1. Follow the damn course (seriously, at least half of the issues I see in this group and on Q&A calls are from people trying to deviate from what the Twins/Alex/Dan teach)
2. Get into a mastermind group and commit to it
3. Fall in love with your customer's problems rather than your solution (shoutout Dewan Bayney for that one)
4. Don't be afraid to ask questions
5. If you haven't hit $10,000/month you don't have business problems, only personal problems that manifest in your business

Revenue Breakdown:
KDP $20,133.21

Ingramspark: $199.06
ACX: $2,000 at the low end

Also did $28,702 in backend sales

Total revenue: $51,104

And just a quick reminder that this is the greatest business on planet right now, we are all so blessed to be able to learn from Christian Mikkelsen Rasmus Mikkelsen Alex Kerr Daniel Locke Kim Petersen and the entire AIA team.

Chase hasn't touched his publishing business in over a year as he decided to dedicate his time and energy on a new business instead. He says, "I haven't touched my publishing business in over 12 months and I've still made $150K this year! Single greatest starter business there is. I have moved on to other things thanks to the freedom."

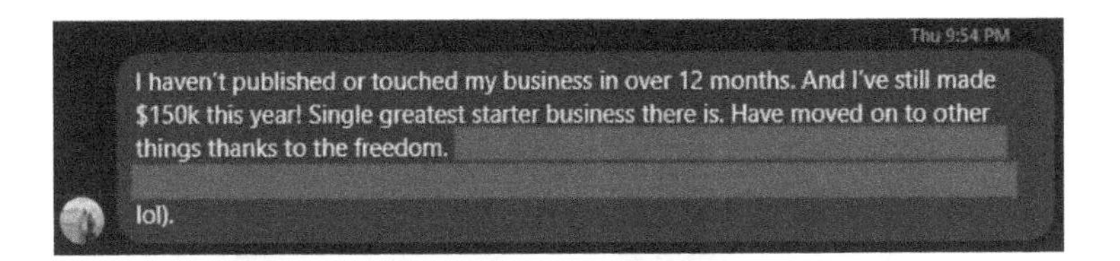

Daniel from the UK (mentioned in Chapter 36) was one of the fastest AIA students to go from $0 to $10,000 in one month in just six months. He is now a coach with us and his #1 focus is helping students get life-changing results with publishing. Thanks for everything you do, Dan. We truly could not have anyone better on our side.

Nick, the community manager at AIA, found success very quickly when he first started publishing in 2020. His best month has been over $5,000. He later began publishing books about his greatest passion in life. The first one was a huge success as it's already making $1,000+ per month. We're very excited to see Nick's business grow to huge heights in the next year. Thanks for your amazing contribution to the community and the company, Nick!

Emeka, a good friend of ours since we first started publishing, has been making full time income from his publishing business for many years and recently decided to sell it for $191,250.

Amount
191,250.00

Send on
Jun 29, 2021

Deliver by
Jun 30, 2021

Addendum

Transaction number

Anthony and Taig are friends that started their publishing business together and their first couple of books are smashing it. They've also landed some well-paying consulting gigs through their books from readers reaching out to get more help from them. Although it's not discussed within this book, that's another great opportunity to create more income streams from your books.

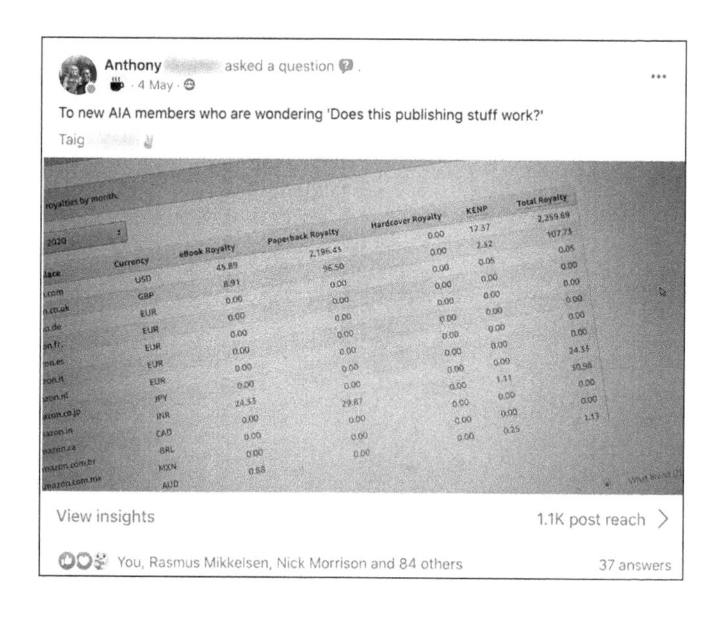

Brock was able to quit his job and travel due to the income from his publishing business. He has also been inducted into the AIA 10K Club.

Brock

12 November 2020 ·

10K club!!

Recieved my award and just want to say a big thanks to the twins.

Hitting 10K/month was my first big business goal i set, I even had it as my phone screen saver for a year until I hit it (it's attached for proof)

Publishing has been such a rollercoaster ride for me but I wouldnt change a thing. It enabled me to quit my job 3 years ago and recently move out of home so I'm super grateful to have found the business and stick it out.

This shit works! Just finish the course from A-Z and stay consistent.

Thanks Rasmus Mikkelsen and Christian Mikkelsen

Carmine has published six books in his first year in AIA, two of which have become bestsellers.

Hello to all AIA Members,

It is about a year now that I have joined AIA and I want to share my results thus far.

Work and business has kept me extremely busy and I've been doing AIA at about 25%, and with that said, I still managed to produce 7 books (2 more are in the progress of being produced) and I have published 6 books!

My books are generating on average $5000 per month. My first book has had the #1 Bestseller status from day one (it's nearly a year now)! My 3rd book has also become a #1 Bestseller since it was launched at the end of last year. My 5th book is also making lots of noise. It's weird that books 1, 3, and 5 (odd numbers) are rocking'n rolling for me lol, I hope book 7 will become another bestseller! This makes me insanely excited because every author's dream is to have that recognition! Now just imagine if I would do this business full time....

All this, just to say, AIA does work!!! If you follow the step-by-step formula that the twins and their team teach you, you will succeed!!!

I wish everyone who has joined AIA lots of success! Remember, this is NOT a race, it's a marathon. Enjoy your journey towards success, at your own pace!

Damian shared his story in our Facebook community to inspire others that if we can do it, so can you! He says he averages about $9,500 USD per month.

Damian
30 August 2020 ·

Persistence is Key you WILL get results just keep going and improving! Hi Just wanted to share my quick story not to brag just to inspire really. 🙂 I started publishing books in 2016 and in some years I've published more and in some less. I can say, between year 1-2 my royalty income hovered around 3,500 USD a month.
Later on, within year 2-3 it hovered at around 6500-7000 USD monthly. Then, after discovering AIA, via what I contribute to the Amazon Ads training and applying, as well as improving descriptions and some cover improvements on existing books, I consistently have gotten it over 10,500 per month with on average about 1,200 spent on Amazon ads. (I wasn't running ads before). So around 9,500 USD profit is average at the moment.
So I can say AIA has improved my profit at least $2500 per month even without publishing further books. (I've just started with Audiobooks, this data is just referring to print, Kindle, and ebook editions).
Note: I publish on Lightningsource first (Which is Ingram- the same as Ingram Spark really, then the same print book on KDP print, then the kindle, then Streetlib for ebooks for Apple, Kobo, Barnes and Noble, etc). My best month to date has been the June KDP / May Lightningsource - so combined royalties for a 30 day period which was paid in Aug 2020 (LSI has one more month delay), which was $11,389 - $1218 in ad spend. So $10,171 in profit, after ads. In the last 5 months it's hovered around there - 9.5K - 10K a month after ads - though, so I'm excited 🙂 I'm attaching some screenshots from this period not to brag at all just to inspire that you CAN get there!
I hope it helps! And, I know this is just the beginning for YOU and ME 🙂

Garry has an incredibly inspiring story. He went from being homeless some years ago to now earning multi-six figures per year just with his audiobooks.

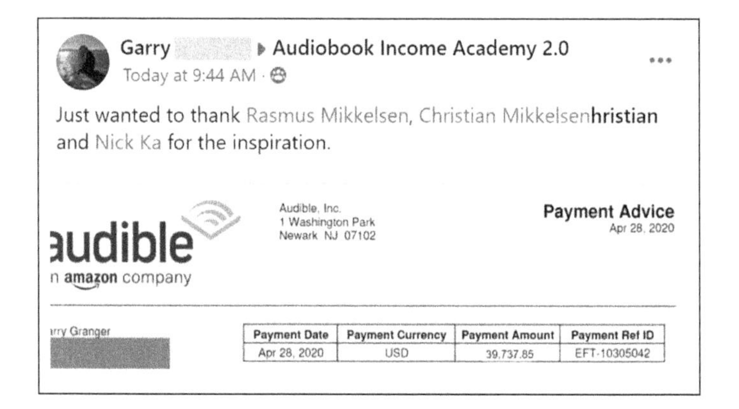

Payment Date	Payment Currency	Payment Amount	Payment Ref ID
Apr 28, 2020	USD	39,737.85	EFT-10305042

Matheus joined as a student in June 2019 and made the following update post 21 months later sharing that he has made over $40,000 in the last 3 months from his publishing business.

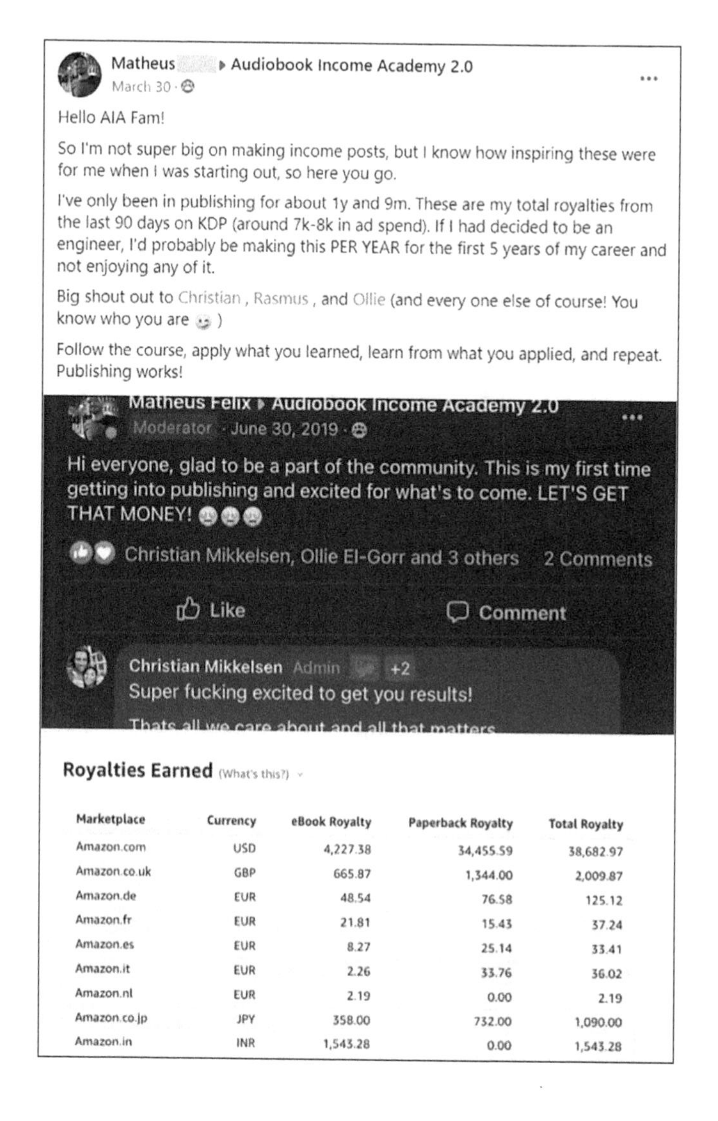

Marketplace	Currency	eBook Royalty	Paperback Royalty	Total Royalty
Amazon.com	USD	4,227.38	34,455.59	38,682.97
Amazon.co.uk	GBP	665.87	1,344.00	2,009.87
Amazon.de	EUR	48.54	76.58	125.12
Amazon.fr	EUR	21.81	15.43	37.24
Amazon.es	EUR	8.27	25.14	33.41
Amazon.it	EUR	2.26	33.76	36.02
Amazon.nl	EUR	2.19	0.00	2.19
Amazon.co.jp	JPY	358.00	732.00	1,090.00
Amazon.in	INR	1,543.28	0.00	1,543.28

Sidd from Australia made this post in our Facebook community to provide some inspiration and motivation for fellow publishers. He said that he started two years ago and generated over $22K in the month of December.

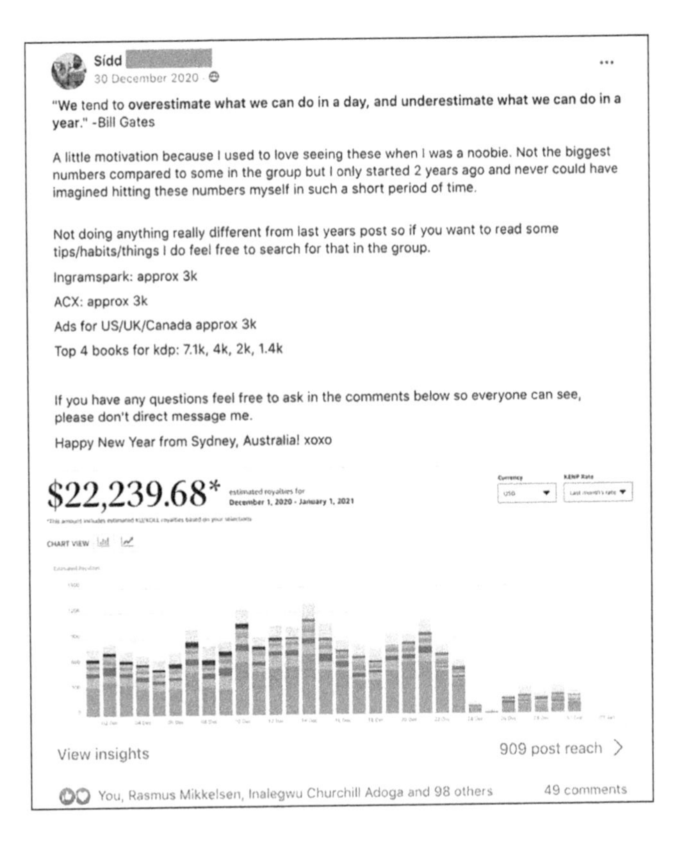
Sidd
30 December 2020

"We tend to **overestimate what we can do in a day, and underestimate what we can do in a year.**" -Bill Gates

A little motivation because I used to love seeing these when I was a noobie. Not the biggest numbers compared to some in the group but I only started 2 years ago and never could have imagined hitting these numbers myself in such a short period of time.

Not doing anything really different from last years post so if you want to read some tips/habits/things I do feel free to search for that in the group.

Ingramspark: approx 3k

ACX: approx 3k

Ads for US/UK/Canada approx 3k

Top 4 books for kdp: 7.1k, 4k, 2k, 1.4k

If you have any questions feel free to ask in the comments below so everyone can see, please don't direct message me.

Happy New Year from Sydney, Australia! xoxo

$22,239.68* estimated royalties for December 1, 2020 - January 1, 2021

CHART VIEW

View insights

909 post reach

You, Rasmus Mikkelsen, Inalegwu Churchill Adoga and 98 others

49 comments

Todd is actually already a very successful businessman, but he was fascinated by the opportunity of passive income from books and audiobooks. He saw it as his ticket to steady income in retirement. While not as big a result as many others, he's very pleased with the first $500 his first book has made.

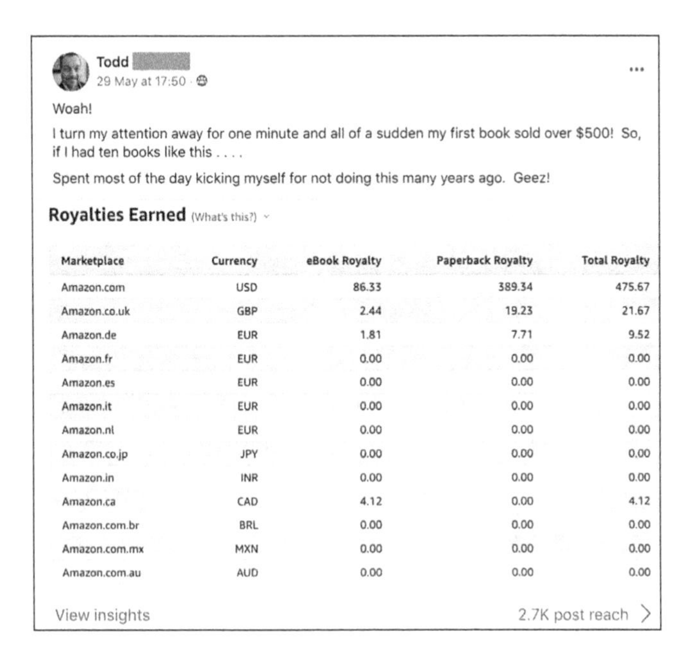

Todd
29 May at 17:50

Woah!

I turn my attention away for one minute and all of a sudden my first book sold over $500! So, if I had ten books like this . . . .

Spent most of the day kicking myself for not doing this many years ago. Geez!

Royalties Earned (What's this?)

Marketplace	Currency	eBook Royalty	Paperback Royalty	Total Royalty
Amazon.com	USD	86.33	389.34	475.67
Amazon.co.uk	GBP	2.44	19.23	21.67
Amazon.de	EUR	1.81	7.71	9.52
Amazon.fr	EUR	0.00	0.00	0.00
Amazon.es	EUR	0.00	0.00	0.00
Amazon.it	EUR	0.00	0.00	0.00
Amazon.nl	EUR	0.00	0.00	0.00
Amazon.co.jp	JPY	0.00	0.00	0.00
Amazon.in	INR	0.00	0.00	0.00
Amazon.ca	CAD	4.12	0.00	4.12
Amazon.com.br	BRL	0.00	0.00	0.00
Amazon.com.mx	MXN	0.00	0.00	0.00
Amazon.com.au	AUD	0.00	0.00	0.00

View insights
2.7K post reach

Fred is having great success with his first book and making money much faster than he expected. He has yet to release the audiobook version of his first book which will add an additional stream of passive income for him.

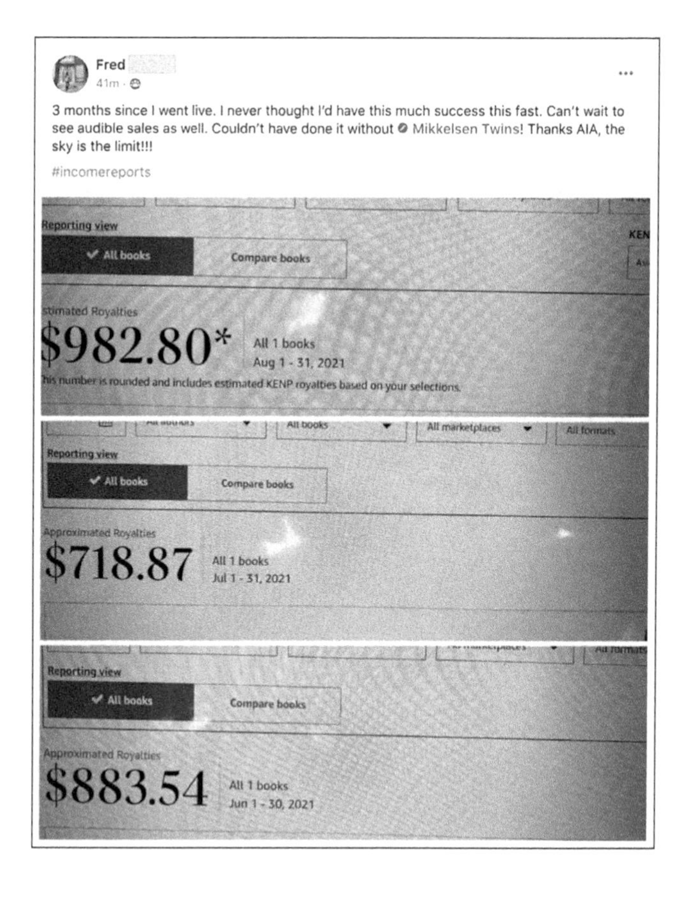

Sarah says her publishing business has been life-changing as it has allowed her to quit her 9-5 job for GOOD. Just one of her books is making about $3,000/month and she's now working on getting more reviews for that book to increase sales even more.

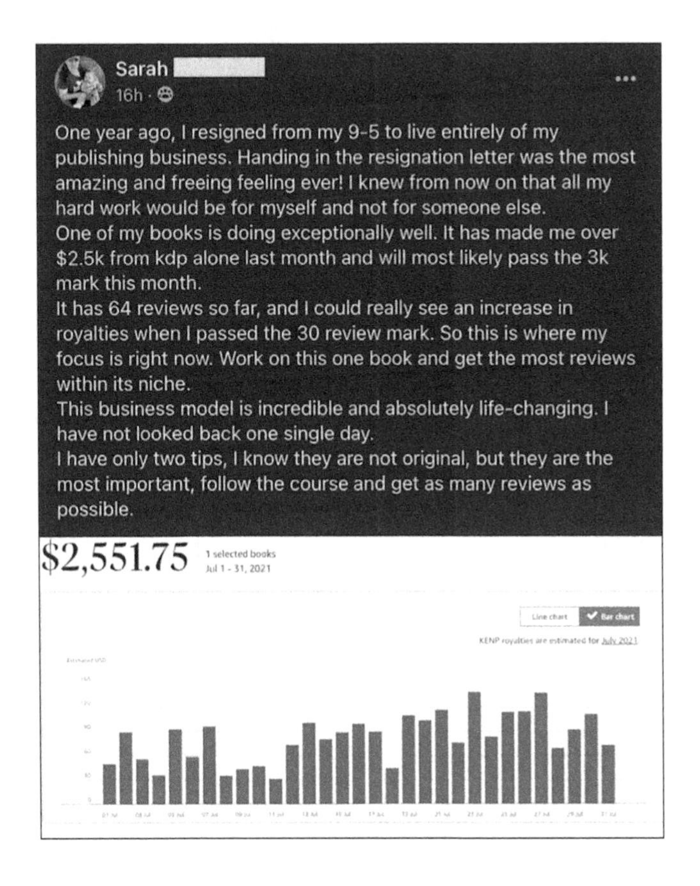

For many more success stories just like this, go to **publishinglife.com/success.**

CONCLUSION

Congratulations! You've completed the first step toward having your own successful publishing business. (Well, unless you just skipped to the end, in which case it's time to go back to the beginning and read this all the way through.)

Most people never finish the books they pick up and start to read, so we really appreciate and value the time you put into reading this book.

I want to leave you with what I believe to be the most powerful quote on planet earth. It's simple and seemingly obvious, but if you embody this and live it, then nothing can ever get in your way.

> "You never fail until you stop trying."
>
> —Albert Einstein

There is nothing you can do to prevent challenges and hardships on your journey. The true difference between those who win at life and those who lose is whether YOU decide to let those things stop you.

I hope this will be a turning point for you in your life. It's up to you to make it happen.

Good luck.

Twins out!

YOUR BONUSES ALL IN ONE PLACE

This book comes with a lot of bonus video content. Instead of scrambling through the book to locate all of the bonus videos, you can find them here—all in one easy-to-access place.

56-minute interview with the most successful AIA audiobook publisher:
Publishinglife.com/patrick

Video training about how to determine demand of any book niche:
Publishinglife.com/niche

Video training about the different ghostwriting options that are available and our recommended ghostwriting companies:
Publishinglife.com/writing

Video training about our recommended cover designers for less than $20 and our go-to cover design service:
Publishinglife.com/covers

24-minute interview with Soorej, who shares his rags-to-riches success story and all the challenges he had to overcome:
Publishinglife.com/soorej

57-minute interview with Trevor about how he built his publishing business, sold it for 6-figures, and lives a lifestyle of travel:
Publishinglife.com/trevor

WORK WITH US

If you would like to start making passive income with your own books and audiobooks and you'd like to have expert guidance from us and our team, go to:

Publishinglife.com/learnmore

On the page, you can select a time to attend the webinar which will provide additional video training along with details about how to join our premium coaching program.

ACKNOWLEDGMENTS

There's a big handful of people that we absolutely need to shout out here because none of this would have been possible without them. I'm talking about this book and the business we've built, which has made every single one of our wildest dreams come true.

While we have worked very hard, we have also been extremely lucky to have stumbled upon this opportunity and the following amazing people. Grateful doesn't even begin to describe how we feel.

Thank you Mom, Dad, Celine, and Camilla for setting us up for success and giving us every opportunity to chase what we really wanted. You don't get to pick your family, but we truly couldn't have been any luckier.

Thank you Stefan James—you are the person who introduced us to the world of self-publishing and online business back in 2016. Without your videos on YouTube, who in the world knows what else we would have gotten ourselves into instead.

Thank you Ollie for writing the foreword to this book, for being a publishing success story even though you did it all without our help, and for hopping on a call with me at any moment when I was stuck on what to write. How do you always have the answer?! And for literally being the funniest person I know. #Finnbolone.

Thank you Emeka, for showing us how to put together an online course and allowing us to launch AIA at your mastermind event in 2018. What a crazy day that was!

Thank you Charlotte Mikkelsen for marrying one of us and creating a badass cover for this book!

Thank you Laura Mikkelsen for marrying the other one and being the best CEO of Publishing Life Services!

Thank you Sam Ovens for teaching the mindset and business philosophies needed to be successful in the online education industry. Your videos changed us into the people we needed to be.

Thank you Alex Becker for teaching us how to use YouTube to grow our company. Without your help, we'd still be stuck trying to figure out how this whole advertising thing works. For anyone that's annoyed at seeing our faces over and over on YouTube ... Sorry! It just works.

Thank you Jason Fladlien for bestowing your webinar expertise upon us. You are the most entertaining and talented marketer there is and the GOAT of webinars.

Thank you Dan, Shahmir, Churchill, Hannah, Nick, and the rest of the growing PublishingLife team for supporting our vision and growing PublishingLife with us. Thank you so much for your continued commitment to the company.

Thank you Dan Henry for being the sole reason that we decided to write this book. Without your guidance, I would have had no idea how to write a book like this that can be the face of our business.

Thank you Alex and Leila Hormozi for believing in us, taking us under your wing, and helping us grow PublishingLife to that NEXT level. We cannot put a price on everything we have already learned from you both.

Thank you Lori Lynn for turning this book into something I'm very proud of and for being so fun to work with! Your passion for writing has rubbed off on me and has made this entire book process truly fun and enjoyable.

Lastly, thank you to all our students and supporters. I still can't believe the amount of people that support two stupid twins on the internet. Our goal is to inspire you to also say to the average, dull life everyone expects of you and chase the unknown, risky and exciting side of life. We sincerely hope we've been able to change your lives for the better, even if it's only a fraction of how much you have changed ours.

ABOUT THE AUTHORS

Rasmus and Christian Mikkelsen (also known as the Mikkelsen Twins) are identical twin brothers and the founders of PublishingLife.com, a multi-million-dollar education company that teaches everyday people how to make money online by creating and publishing books and audiobooks.

Rasmus started his work career as a Chinese food delivery driver and Christian as a receptionist at a physical therapy office. It didn't take long for them to realize that any "normal" career path was not for them. Working 9–5 at a sh*tty job means living paycheck-to-paycheck and giving away all your freedom, and that is not their definition of a happy life.

In their pursuit to find a way to make money outside of a job, they came across book publishing as a business model. They hired writers, cover designers, and narrators to create books for them, then they would publish them as ebooks, print books, and audiobooks on Amazon and Audible. This completely changed their lives.

They started traveling all over the world and shared what they were doing on YouTube. People started watching their videos, publishing books, and making passive income, too. They've now served over 10,000+ clients and have been recognized in *Forbes* and *Entrepreneur Magazine* for their work.

CPSIA information can be obtained
at www.ICGtesting.com
Printed in the USA
LVHW012148061222
734737LV00014B/1506